THE OFFICIAL IDENTITY THEFT PREVENTION HANDBOOK

Everyone's Identity Has Already Been Stolen
– Learn What You Can Do About It

DENIS G. KELLY

Sterling & Ross Publishers
NEW YORK

Published by
Sterling & Ross Publishers
New York, NY 10001
www.sterlingandross.com

For bulk or special sales, contact specialsales@sterlingandross.com

Library of Congress Cataloging-in-Publication Data

Kelly, Denis G.
The official identity theft prevention handbook / by Denis G. Kelly.
p. cm.
ISBN 978-0-9827588-2-3 (pbk.)
1. Identity theft--United States--Handbooks, manuals, etc. 2. Identity theft-
-United States--Prevention--Handbooks, manuals, etc. I. Title.
HV6679.K45 2011
332.024--dc22
2010043068

Cover design: Nederpelt Media.
Book design: Rachel Trusheim.

10 9 8 7 6 5 4 3 2 1

Printed in the United States of America.

To all those victims and families whose lives have been turned upside down through no fault of their own. I wrote this book so that others might learn.

Acknowledgments

First and foremost, I thank my dad, DK1, for putting up with me and my ideas (and the results of said ideas). I owe my mom, Jean Ann Kelly, gratitude for providing inspiration, creativity and selflessness in a world often absorbed in the opposite. And my stepmom, Grace Kelly, helped me develop my writing skills such that what was once a weakness blossomed into a strength.

I would be remiss if I did not extend a special thanks to my publisher, Drew Nederpelt, and executive editor, Rachel Trusheim. They took a chance on me and worked relentlessly to bring this book to life. They were early adopters of *The Movement*, and I will forever appreciate their sound direction and patience.

We all cross paths with teachers who inspire us to do better or choose doors that would be otherwise in our blind spots, and I am no exception. While there are many teachers who provided such guidance, the following teachers provided me an *extra* nudge in the right direction. From Naperville North High School: Mr. Yarbrough, Mr. Foerch, Mr. Petersen and Mr. and Mrs. Martin. From Marquette University: Dr. Daniels and Dr. Mandell.

I owe a special debt of gratitude to John "Jack" Goeken and John E. Hughes, two American corporate mavericks and titans. While still a struggling student at Marquette University with few notable successes, these gentlemen took the time to teach me valuable life and business lessons including that corporate America is not always right. When there are injustices or a better way of doing things, it is up to you to prove it. The lessons learned from these two will always be a motivator and serve as a guiding light.

I credit my friend Julian Tellier for being there and trusting in me when there were few. And I am especially indebted to my friend John Trautman for being the first to recognize and support the necessity of bringing identity theft education and training to a much larger audience.

The lifelong support and moral compass provided by my family with names of Kelly, Grimes, Rapach and Vandenplas has given me the courage to fight the status quo and defend those without a voice.

Finally, I appreciate the warm-heartedness of the staff and patrons of Starbucks on Lincoln Road in Miami Beach where I spent a majority of my time writing *The Handbook*.

Contents

 Introduction

What is America's *top-ranked* crime concern? Identity theft. According to a 2009 Gallup poll, 66 percent of adults in the United States worry "frequently" or "occasionally" about being a victim of identity theft. Why is the percentage of adults concerned with identity theft more than *three times* greater than the percentage concerned with "being sexually assaulted" or "getting murdered"? Because identity theft in America is a common, elusive and potentially devastating crime. This Gallup poll demonstrates that Americans understand the world we are in: it's the Wild, Wild West where identity criminals operate with little resistance and your personally identifying information is constantly at risk.

Let's take a look at Todd Davis, CEO of LifeLock, who was made infamous for an advertising campaign in which he nationally broadcasted his real Social Security number because his company *guaranteed* that his identity would not be stolen. Not only was his identity stolen, it was reportedly stolen 13 times.

That's right, 13 times. The reality is that due to changing technology, human actions and an imperfect system, no company or service can *guarantee* that your identity will not be stolen. Not only did LifeLock's CEO broadcast his Social Security number, but the company doubled down by marketing a guarantee: "We're so confident, we back our clients with a $1 million guarantee." What CEO Todd Davis failed to inform us was that this was a "guarantee of service" and not a guarantee that your identity would not be stolen. Your identity could still be stolen while having LifeLock. This guarantee was a complete fleece job.

As a result, LifeLock was fined $12 million by the Federal Trade Commission in 2010 for their transgressions and for misleading the American public, which is equivalent to a slap on the wrist compared to the astronomical amount of profits being generated by this company.

The situation exacerbated consumers' problems with LifeLock, given that in 2009 the global information and credit services giant Experian entered the identity protection battle and sued LifeLock for providing fraud alerts for their subscribers. Their basis for the suit was a technicality in the verbiage contained in the Fair Credit Reporting Act, claiming that "companies" are not legally authorized to execute fraud alerts on behalf of the consumers as the act states this process is only allowed to be performed by "individuals." A summary judgment in May 2009, made by an activist judge with highly controversial (and I believe irrational) reasoning, sided with Experian.

Now why would Experian oppose a company that was executing fraud alerts on the behalf of consumers with their full knowledge and authority? A fraud alert essentially requires credit issuers to take an additional step to validate that the "applicant is who he or she claims to be." Common sense would dictate that this must be a normal part of the credit-issuing process, but do not forget that our existing identity system is warped and common sense is considered "N/A." However, fraud alerts make the process of extending credit more costly, and this costs credit information services companies, like Experian, money. More importantly, setting a fraud alert opts the consumer out of prescreened offers of credit and insurance. In other words, Experian can no longer sell your personal data (which you never agreed to allow them to sell in the first place), and that also costs them a lot more money. Experian contends that the fraud alerts are only intended for real victims of identity theft. Imagine if ADT stated that you couldn't get an alarm system until *after* your house was burglarized. Well, that's exactly what's happening in the identity theft prevention industry.

By virtue of this controversial ruling, LifeLock and companies with similar identity theft prevention models had to modify their services to less-valuable *detection* measures. The one thing LifeLock was actually doing right was providing effective identity theft *prevention* services. Were they perfect, or did they protect against *all* types of identity theft? Of course not—no such service exists in the current structure of the industry. However, these basic defense tactics eliminated an incredible amount of "would be" identity theft incidents. Many people who had a former LifeLock safeguard to validate that "they are who they say they are" when applying for credit no longer have this protection.

It didn't stop here. LifeLock adjusted its business model such that its most valuable service, placing fraud alerts, is no longer offered; however, $12 million was not enough to stop them from deceptively marketing their product. At the time of this writing, LifeLock's home page places a "check mark" next to "fraud alerts placed with the credit bureaus," but on the "How LifeLock Works" page (http://www.lifelock.com/services/compare), there is no mention of these phantom fraud alerts. I sent an e-mail to LifeLock's Member Services to clarify this discrepancy, and I received no response.

There is a video on LifeLock's website that states: "We are LifeLock, and we believe you have the right to live life without having to think twice every time you fill out a form, make a purchase or throw out your mail."[1]

This is patently wrong. As you will discover in this book, regardless of which identity theft protection service you have, you *better* think twice *every* time you do *anything* if it potentially compromises your sensitive personally identifying information. As evidenced in the LifeLock example above, identity theft protection entities diminished their services and still inform you that you do not need to be concerned with identity theft if you have their service. And even worse, in a non-scientific poll, I discovered nearly everyone with LifeLock's service has no clue about what is actually included, and they believe LifeLock offers the best identity theft *prevention* service around!

Fool me once, shame on you; fool me twice, shame on me.

I witnessed the rapid expansion of the identity theft industry from "the inside." As a partner at a national mortgage bank, I handed over cases of rampant fraud to the FBI. At some point, the criminals were so bold as to place an ad in a local Eastern-European newspaper looking to purchase identities. At least these were the "nice criminals" whose identity theft and/or fraud did not cause pain to the consumer but merely defrauded our largest institutions out of billions of dollars. This is the component of the *subprime meltdown* that is routinely dismissed. The government was so woefully unprepared to enforce the identity theft laws it

---

1 "Home Page." LifeLock. September 13, 2010. http://www.life-lock.com/?v=13

enacted. Certainly there were other main contributions to the subprime meltdown, but this component rarely receives the attention it deserves.

I observed firsthand how identity theft ruined the lives of individuals and was tearing our society apart. I thought it was such a senseless crime that could be substantially controlled with relatively simple actions. I understood that it could not easily be completely eliminated, but these *simple actions* would certainly significantly decrease the number of incidents and pain caused to individuals and society.

I reached my tipping point in 2009 when I understood the following:

1. The government either does not have the will, knowledge or capabilities to take the lead on this task.

2. Closely related entities (i.e., identity theft defense companies, credit bureaus) were slipping to a point whereby the existence of identity theft actually improved their returns, and they were making policy decisions accordingly.

3. No company or individual had the unique knowledge and experience necessary to effectively address this societal issue.

I did not choose to write this book; it had to be written. It is time for our society to have an identity awakening or this issue will turn into an *epidemic*... Identity theft is a now a foregone conclusion and not a crime we feel confident we can prevent. I understand this book is not going to be the entire solution in itself, but we have to place a stick in the sand. *The Official Identity Theft Prevention Handbook* may make me the target of some very powerful institutions and individuals, but I am willing to jump on this *identity grenade*. My primary armament is something lacking on the other side: the truth.

The Official Identity Theft Prevention Handbook is the first book to consider identity theft in its proper context. I will walk you through a step-by-step process teaching you how you can best protect yourself. The government and corporate America have proven they cannot effectively protect you; so, we need to organize an effort at the individual and community levels to span the gap. Most importantly, I prove that everybody's identity has already been stolen. It is only with this understanding that both individuals and society can effectively combat this crime.

I have made it my mission to properly educate, train and protect the American citizen from identity theft. In addition to this book, I have developed related entities to help me achieve this goal. The Identity Ambassador Commission, whose motto is "Educo. Exercito. Munimen." (Educate. Train. Protect.), originated the F.A.C.T.S. principle, which states that all identity theft education and training must be "Free. Accurate. Current. Transparent. Shared." The Commission developed a rigorous training course with a high testing standard; upon successful completion, the individual is designated as a Certified Identity Expert (CIE). All CIEs are required to abide by a strict code of ethics. The Commission distributes a free monthly newsletter to keep consumers aware and educated.

Identity Safe Cities (ISC) is an organization with the goal of increasing participation and awareness of identity theft in order to decrease the number of incidents and reduce the losses incurred by identity theft victims. ISC takes a partnership approach with the cities as we recognize that our joint goal cannot be achieved without substantial participation. Included in the ISC Certification is a full-day visit and assessment by a specially trained CIE. The ISC significantly assists with our community outreach initiative.

TheIDChannel.com is a centralized, dependable, comprehensive and timely resource of identity theft news and information. It is an informative, educational medium that encourages community interaction and participation. Most consumers cannot find valuable identity theft information through traditional online search tactics; there are mountains of erroneous and irrelevant news stories. At TheIDChannel. com we sift through this information to make certain the content is relevant and accurate. Membership is free.

IDCuffs.com provides a convenience service for executing identity theft prevention tactics. Due to the lawsuit by Experian, IDCuffs.com is unable to perform these tasks on behalf of the consumer; however, this is a reminder service to make certain that *you* are performing the critical tasks at the appropriate times. It is important to note that you do not *need* this service to perform the tasks, but we have discovered many forget or give up on these tasks because of their busy lives. The service also includes an invaluable, proprietary online tool for use in the unfortunate event that you become a victim of identity theft.

I bring all of these initiatives to your attention right from the beginning because I believe in full transparency. There are profit motivations for these initiatives, but I have designed the programs to maximize benefits to individuals and society while providing a fair return to those involved. I instituted checks and balances to make certain the structures are not exploitative of this awful crime. This is not to say that some unsavory individuals will not sneak in underneath the radar, but we will do our best to keep these entities operating at a level that is the *gold standard of ethical behavior.* Unlike the other organizations that operate in this space, my motivations are to eradicate this crime, and there will be no happier day in my life then when these organizations and companies are shut down because they are no longer needed. I dream of a utopian society where identity theft *cannot* occur. I hope to bring us closer to this dream.

I have said much in this introduction but little about the actual book you're about to read. This was intentional. It is important you have proper context and understanding of my motivations first and foremost. With that said, *The Official Identity Theft Prevention Handbook* provides *substantially everything* you need to know to give yourself the best opportunity to avoid identity theft. I state *substantially everything* because I know that effective prevention is a continuous process that requires your participation. I have presented all of the information in an easy-to-understand format to maximize the value of your takeaways and to show you how to employ these tactics immediately.

Identity theft protection starts with personal accountability. Identity theft protection is similar to insurance: most people understand the need for it only *after* it's too late. *The Official Identity Theft Prevention Handbook* is the **only** book that provides the facts. Once you've completed this book, you will have the instructions to a magic wand; the rest is up to you.

Safe Identities,
Denis

 # Chapter 1

The History of Identity Theft and Social Security Numbers

On August 14, 1935, President Franklin D. Roosevelt signed into law the Social Security Act, and a great compact with society began. Unknowingly, the foundation had been laid for one of the greatest challenges of the next century: identity theft. According to a report by the United States Department of Justice, "Identity theft has become perhaps the defining crime of the information age."[2] The reason the Department of Justice makes this claim is because the data supports the conclusion that everyone is already a victim of identity theft.[3]

There is an identity stolen every three seconds[4], and there have been *more* records compromised via data breaches since 2005 than the entire U.S. population.[5]

---

2   "Identity Theft – A Research Review." National Institute of Justice, The Research, Development, and Evaluation Agency of the U.S. Department of Justice. p 1. July 2007.

3   It is important to note that not every victim realizes he or she has been subjected to identity theft and/or suffers actual damages.

4   "2010 Identity Fraud Survey Report: Identity Fraud Continues to Rise – New Accounts Fraud Drives Increase; Consumer Costs at an All-Time Low." Javelin Strategy & Research. p 8. February 2010.

5   "Chronology of Data Breaches." Privacy Rights Clearinghouse. 500,000,000 breaches from January 1, 2005 to August 26, 2010.

Since 2000, Americans have been inundated with news stories, commercials and personal experiences regarding identity theft. The average person understands on a higher level the seriousness and the enormity of the issue; however, few understand the history, the laws, the perpetrators and consequently what can be done to mitigate the risks both on a societal and personal level. The same sources that have raised the awareness level of identity theft have also added to the confusion. There are journalists who do not understand the full scope or intricacies of the crime, there are companies that seek to exploit this epidemic through deceptive advertising and there are well-rooted institutions with economic advantages of allowing identity theft to proliferate, all of which have elevated an inherently complex subject to a virtually unsolvable puzzle.

The Identity Ambassador Commission terms this puzzle "the exponential, multi-dimensional challenge."[6]

Liberty is only achieved in concert with the rule of law. From terrorism to bank scandals to common criminal acts, the ability to enforce the rule of law is being challenged to its core due to identity theft. You cannot fight what you cannot see, and identity theft is a faceless crime. The right to pursue liberty is being egregiously undermined, and the threat is growing.

The stakes are high, but the signs are promising. Society has taken many positive steps to eradicate this nuisance. This is society's problem, and its resolution requires many different and often competing agents to work together. The Identity Ambassador Commision contributes to this battle by providing effective, free education and training to all.

---

6   Identity Ambassador Commission. <http://identityambassa-dor.org/>

The History of Identity Theft

Identity theft has been present in various forms since the beginning of mankind. The oldest recorded case occurred in 1930 BC when Jacob stole his older brother Esau's identity to obtain the blessing of his father, Isaac. While near death and unable to see, Isaac requested Esau to hunt and prepare a special meal for him and then he would give him the special blessing. Jacob deceived Isaac by convincing him that he was Esau, and the blessing was bestowed upon him. Esau asked Isaac to bless him too, and Isaac replied that there were no blessings left. At least nowadays, in the case of credit card identity theft, the consumer's loss is normally limited to $50 and not an eternal blessing!

As societies have evolved from a predominant relationship structure of *one-to-few* to *one-to-many*, identities have become easier to steal. The best defense of personal validation of your identity is achieved through this societal structure (i.e., neighbors with whom you were raised would validate your identity). The purpose of identity theft has remained the same: gain something of value by utilizing (or creating) another's identity and use it as though it were you own. In fact, fraudulent claims and documents were used to gain citizenship into Rome similarly as they are used today to gain citizenship into the United States. However, the process has changed: citizenship records in Roman times were verified personally, and the punishment for falsification was death! In the modern-day United States, with little money and the proper connections, noncitizens can assume a U.S. citizen's identity with relative ease[7], and there is typically no punishment bestowed upon the actual identity thief.[8]

The shift to a one-to-many society requires a different identity system and specifically requires the development of a national identity system—one that has *enforceable restrictions* in place in order to effectively control the threat and proliferation of identity theft.[9] Such an identifier was never developed, and an insecure Social Security number system has been adopted as the default unique identifier.

There are credible arguments and forces that have prevented the development of a national ID system. Specifically, opponents argue that it violates civil liberties. Ironically, the main goal of a national ID system is to protect such freedoms. Ultimately, society needs to weigh the costs and benefits of all possible solutions to determine which system provides the *optimal* protection of liberty.

The issue has compounded since the uses of identity theft expanded beyond blessings and citizenship to bank fraud, terrorism and medical fraud (to name a few). The perfect storm developed as the value of identity theft increased, the costs decreased and the risks became relatively low. From a criminal's perspective, why not commit a crime with a high return that is relatively simple and chances of getting caught are low? This combination presents society

---

7   Statement of Michael Everitt, Unit Chief, ICE Forensic Document Laboratory, United States Department of Homeland Security to Senate Committee on the Judiciary Subcommittee on Terrorism. Technology and Homeland Security. May 2, 2007.

8   From April 2006 through January 2010, United States Immigration and Customs Enforcement division handling immigration fraud had only 1,493 convictions. <http://www.ice.gov/pi/news/factsheets/070301dbfi.htm>

9   "Privacy Impact Study." REAL ID Act Proposed Rule. United States Department of Homeland Security. p 7. March 1, 2007.

with the *exponential, multi-dimensional challenge.*

How Social Security Numbers Morphed into a National Identifier

The shift from an agricultural to industrial society as well the economic crisis of the Great Depression was a combined impetus for creating a social safety net for American citizens. During the Industrial Revolution, the percentage of Americans living in cities dramatically increased, and by the year 1920, for the first time in our nation's history, more people were living in cities than on farms.[10]

This contributed to the disappearance of the *extended family* and transition to the *nuclear family.* The extended family structure traditionally provided support when a family member became too old or infirm to work. Additionally, from 1900–1930, the average life span in America increased 10 years, which is the most rapid increase in life span in recorded human history. This created a unique societal issue of a rapid increase in the number of people with no means to take care of themselves; and thus, Social Security was born and signed into law by Franklin D. Roosevelt on August 14, 1935.

It is important to note that I make no claim to the validity or importance of the *overall* Social Security system. Furthermore, I do not solely place blame on the Social Security Administration for the explosion of identity theft due to this highly insecure unique identifying system. It was not developed for this purpose, and it was never imagined in the 1930s that it would be used in the future as a national identifier.

---

10 "Brief History." Social Security Administration. <http://www.ssa.gov/history/briefhistory3.html>

FDR Signing the Social Security Act of 1935[11]

The government originally stated that a Social Security number (SSN) would not be a means for identification and made assurances that the use would be limited to Social Security programs such as calculating retirement benefits. According to a United States Government Accountability report, "SSNs have evolved beyond their original intended purpose and have become the identifier of choice for public and private sector entities, and are used for numerous non-Social Security purposes."[12]

It is commonly accepted that a SSN is the de facto unique identifier, and here are some key milestones in its universal adoption:

---

11   "Signing the Social Security Act of 1935." Social Security Online. Composite photograph. <http://www.ssa.gov/history/fdrsign. html>

12   "Social Security Numbers, More Could Be Done to Protect SSNs." United States Government Accountability Office. Testimony Before the Subcommittee on Social Security, Committee on Ways and Means, House of Representatives. p 3. March 30, 2006.

1943   Executive Order 9397 stated that all federal components must use SSNs exclusively whenever it is advisable to set up a new identification system for individuals.

1961   The Civil Service Commission adopted SSNs.

1962   The IRS adopted SSNs as its official taxpayer identification number.

1965   The IRS enacted Medicare and it became necessary for most individuals over 65 to have a SSN.

1966   The Veterans Administration began using SSNs for hospital admissions and patient record keeping.

1969   The Department of Defense adopted SSNs in lieu of military service numbers.

1970   The Bank Records and Foreign Transactions Act (PL 91-508) required all banks, savings and loan associations, credit unions and securities brokers/dealers to obtain SSNs on all of their customers.

1971   The SSA task force published a report recommending mass SSN enumeration in schools and considered cooperating with specific health, education and welfare uses of the SSN by state, local and other nonprofit organizations.

1972   The Social Security Amendments of 1972 (PL 92-603) required SSA to issue SSNs to all legally admitted aliens at entry and to anyone receiving or applying for any benefit paid for by federal funds; required the SSA to obtain evidence to establish age, citizenship, or alien status or identity; and authorized the SSA to enumerate children at the time they first entered school.

1973   The Report by Health, Education and Welfare Secretary's Advisory Committee on Automated Personal Data System concluded that the adoption of a universal identifier by this country was not desirable and found the SSN was not suitable for such a purpose as it does not meet the criteria of a universal identifier that distinguishes a person from all others.

1976   The Tax Reform Act of 1976 (PL 94-455) amended the Social Security Act to allow states the use of SSNs for administration of any tax, general public assistance, driver's license or motor vehicle.

The Federal Advisory Committee on False Identification rejected the idea of a national identifier and did not even consider the SSN for such a purpose.

1977   The Carter administration proposed that the Social Security card be one of the authorized documents by which an employer could be assured that a job applicant could work in this country and also stated that the SSN card should become a national identity document.

1982   The Debt Collection Act (PL 97-365) required all applicants for loans under any federal loan program furnish their SSNs to the agency supplying the loan.

1983   The Interest and Dividend Tax Compliance Act (PL 98-

67) required SSNs for all interest-bearing accounts.

1986   The Tax Reform Act of 1986 (PL 99-514) required individuals filing a tax return of each dependent 5 years or older to provide a SSN.

The Commercial Motor Vehicle Safety Act of 1986 (PL 99-750) authorized the Secretary of Transportation to require the use of the SSN on the commercial motor vehicle operator's license.

The Higher Education Amendments of 1986 (PL 99-498) required that student loan applicants submit their SSN as a condition of eligibility.

1987   The first program enabled parents to obtain a SSN for their newborn infants automatically when the infant's birth was registered with the state. Currently, all 50 states, Washington, D.C. and Puerto Rico participate in the program.

By this point, if you wanted to work, drive, hold a bank account, file taxes, purchase a home, go to school or be a member in the military, it required a SSN and/or unique identifier. As the government increased its use of and dependence upon SSNs as a unique identifier, private institutions were forced either directly or indirectly to follow suit. Ironically, the government continuously rejected the idea of a national identifier and understood that SSNs were not designed for such a function and yet continued to pass laws that forced SSNs to be a national identifier.

The government forced society into a national identification program with all of the shortcomings and risks of such a system without benefits and proper safeguards.

Now we have established beyond question that SSNs serve as a national identity system. This was even reinforced in 2004 by the acting Inspector General of the Social Security Administration, Patrick P. O'Carroll, who said, "I would like to begin my testimony today with a simple declaration: The SSN is a national identifier."[13]

I assert this is not a de facto national identifier, but it is a true and direct national identifying scheme. Albeit there is not a law that specifically states that an *SSN is an official identifier*; however, the aggregate of laws establish this fact and the acceptance of it as an official identifier makes it so. It looks, seems and acts like an official national identifier; therefore it is. For our purposes, whether it is a de facto or direct national identifying system is irrelevant. I raise this claim to refute a common argument that the *government never intended for SSNs to be a national identifier* as history proves the contrary.[14]

The Faults of the Social Security Number as a National Identity Program

You may ask yourself, "What is all the concern about utilizing Social Security numbers as a national identity system?" There are many faults, and the following are the main issues:

1. A universal identity system requires universal legislation to properly develop and safeguard it.

---

13   Patrick P. O'Carroll, acting Inspector General of the Social Security Administration. Testimony to the House Ways and Means Committee's Subcommittee on Social Security. June 15, 2004.

14   I generally believe the SSA did not intend for SSNs to become a national identifier, but the history of legislation since the inception of SSNs proves government *as a whole* intended to make SSNs a national identifier.

2. The numbering system is highly predictable.

3. It does not contain any biometric identifiers.

4. The cards are not tamper-proof.

5. It is utilized both for *identification* and *authentication*.

Let's take a closer look at these issues.

1. A universal identity system requires universal legislation to properly develop and safeguard it.

The main vulnerability of utilizing the Social Security numbers as a national identity system is that it does not have universal legislation that properly safeguards it. To be sure, even with proper laws, the system has fundamental flaws. As Social Security numbers have emerged over time to become the national identifier, these flaws have become exposed, and in some cases laws have been enacted to fill the voids in the system. A report from the Government Accountability Office (GAO) in September 2008 perfectly illustrates this flaw: the GAO estimated that "85 percent of the largest counties make records with full or partial SSNs available in bulk or online and only 16 percent place any restrictions on the types of entities that can obtain these records."[15]

It is impossible to effectively counteract the flaws of the system through legislation for the following reasons:

---

15 "Social Security Numbers Are Widely Available in Bulk and On-line Records, but Changes to Enhance Security are Occurring." United States Government Accountability Office. Letter to the Honorable Charles E. Schumer, Chairman of the Subcommittee on Administrative Oversight and the Courts Committee on the Judiciary, United States Senate. p 3. September 19, 2008.

a. The Social Security number is not recognized as a national identifier. The government constantly goes out of its way to attempt to argue against this fact. If the issue is misdiagnosed from the onset, then it is impossible to draft and pass effective legislation.

b. The crime of identity theft has many different forms and affects many different components in society in many different ways. Commonly the agency most affected by a crime is the lead consultant in developing legislation to appropriately and effectively address the crime (and is also the lead enforcement agency). Because identity theft affects virtually every government agency, every agency has different requirements and thus consults Congress accordingly. In May 2006, President George Bush signed Executive Order 13402, which established the Identity Theft Task Force and "charged 15 federal departments and agencies with crafting a comprehensive national strategy to combat more effectively this pernicious crime [identity theft]."[16] It is frequently difficult to establish jurisdictional authority between two agencies; so, imagine the difficulty in drafting legislation that significantly involves 15 different government federal departments and agencies (and the reality is that many more could have been involved and/or were only indirectly represented).

---

16   The President's Identity Theft Task Force Report. December 2008. p vii.

c. Due to the setup of the Social Security system, the identity theft legislation is normally reactionary. In other words, as a form of identity theft is recognized, a law(s) is passed to address it. Over time, this has presented a quilt of laws. With a proper national identifier system, universal legislation that defines authority, lead agency, legislation flow, communication and enforcement would all be well defined. In its current state, the Social Security Administration is not even the agency most affected by identity theft.

Identity theft is a complicated crime, and thus it is difficult to develop effective laws. The Social Security number is the thieves' main tool as it functions as a national identifier. While many laws have been passed to assist in diminishing the incidents of identity theft, none of the laws are as effective as universal legislation designed specifically for a national identity system.

2. The numbering system is highly predictable.

Many of the flaws of the Social Security number as a unique identifier are based on the fact that it was never designed nor developed to be a unique identifier. SSNs are not completely random, and it is possible to predict, entirely from public data, narrow ranges of values wherein individual SSNs are likely to fall.[17]

The Social Security Administration publishes the general sequence of numbers as follows: the first three

---

17   Alessandro Acquisti and Ralph Gross. "Predicting Social Security numbers from public data." Communicated by Stephen E. Feinberg, Carnegie Mellon University, Pittsburg, PA. May 5, 2009. p 1.

digits are the Area Number (AN), the next two are its Group Number (GN) and the last four are its Serial Number (SN). There is a relationship between ANs and states/ zip codes. Some low population states and U.S. possessions have one AN each, and other states are allocated sets of ANs (New York has 85 possible sequences of ANs). Within each AN, GNs are assigned in a precise but non-consecutive order (the sequence of assigned GNs: 01–09 odd numbers, 10–98 even numbers, 02–08 even numbers, and 11–99 odd numbers).[18] It has been proven that a strong correlation exists between dates of birth and all nine SSN digits.[19]

There are studies that prove the predictability of entire nine digit SSNs within a small range. Even more alarming is that certain entities (such as Credit Reporting Agencies) often only require seven digits to be correct for validation since there are errors and inconsistencies on consumer credit reports.[20]

The lack of randomness to the assignment, which leads to its predictability, needlessly increases the insecurity of the overall system as a unique identifier. An entirely new system is required for a secure national identifier scheme; however, a short-term solution that mitigates the risk posed by the predictability of SSNs is to change the assignment such that they are entirely random.

---

18   Social Security Administration. "History." <http://www.ssa. gov/history/ssn/geocard.html>

19   Alessandro Acquisti and Ralph Gross. "Predicting Social Security numbers from public data." Communicated by Stephen E. Feinberg, Carnegie Mellon University, Pittsburg, PA. May 5, 2009.

20   Federal Trade Commission. "Report to Congress under sections 318 and 319 of the Fair and Accurate Credit Transactions Act of 2003." 2004. p 39. <http://www.ftc.gov/reports/facta/041209factarpt.pdf>

3. It does not contain any biometric identifiers.

Biometrics are unique physical traits such as fingerprints, face recognition, DNA, palm prints, hand geometry and iris recognition. It is commonly accepted that a secure national identifying scheme must contain biometrics. To be sure, biometrics should not be relied upon solely as it has its own limitations and faults. For example, the first step when utilizing biometrics is *enrollment*. This is the initial process of gathering and storing the biometric information of the individual. If fraudulent information is provided at the enrollment stage, then the subsequent authentications would also fail to detect the perpetrator because the biometrics would be a match. *Bad information in results in bad information out.*

As with all components of a national identity system, there are concerns regarding civil liberties and biometrics, and these concerns need to be addressed and balanced. However, the SSN operating as a unique identifier without utilizing biometrics is an unsecure system.

4. The cards are not tamper-proof.

In addition to including biometrics, the cards must be counterfeit-proof or, minimally, the cards need to be difficult to counterfeit. Counterfeit protections were first introduced to Social Security cards in 1983, and the latest changes were implemented in October 2007 as a result of the Intelligence Reform and Terrorism Prevention Act of 2004. The improvements include a unique non-repeating design that makes it difficult or impossible to change the information listed on the card. There are also color-shifting inks (similar to what is used in currency) and a latent image that is visible only when viewed at specific angles. While these changes are improvements and makes counterfeiting slightly beyond the skills of a knowledgeable computer kid, they are relatively low hurdles for sophisticated counterfeiters.

The effectiveness of the improvements is further diminished by the SSA policy, which allows previous versions of the card to be utilized! In fact, there are over 50 valid versions of the card, many with little or no counterfeiting protection.[21] If less than 10 percent of the cards in circulation have the latest counterfeit-reducing measures and it is possible to counterfeit cards that do not have these measures (since previous versions are still valid), it is readily apparent that the Social Security cards are easy to counterfeit.

Social Security Cards

5. It is utilized both for *identification* and *authentication*.

Identification matches an individual with his or her

---

21   "SOCIAL SECURITY ADMINISTRATION – Improved Agency Coordination Needed for Social Security Card Enhancement Efforts." United States Government Accountability Office. Report to the Chairman, Committee on the Judiciary, House of Representatives. March 2006. p 7.

records and authentication verifies that he or she is who he or she claims to be. Identifiers are widely known (i.e., first and last name), whereas authenticators are effective only when secret (and thus not widely known). Commenters at a Federal Trade Commision (FTC) SSN Workshop stated, "SSNs do not function well as authenticators because they are used commonly as identifiers and thus are widely available."[22]

An authenticating factor should be something a person:

• Knows (like a password or PIN)

• Has (like a physical device or token)

• Is (a physical characteristic like a fingerprint—biometrics)

SSNs are being utilized far less as "sole authenticators." Most entities have realized the inherent risk of utilizing a SSN by itself as an authenticator. However, a SSN may be used to facilitate other forms of authentication such as knowledge-based questioning. While progress has been made in reducing SSNs' use as both identifiers and authenticators, there is still much left to do.

So now we can see that there is enormous evidence of the limitations and risks posed by utilizing the SSN as a national identifier. The commenters at the FTC SSN Workshop also stated that the "widespread use and availability of SSNs cannot be completely reversed and to 'put the genie

---

22   FTC Staff Summary, at 26-27; Transcript of SSN Workshop (December 10, 2007) at 184-85. Remarks of Dr. Annie I. Anton, Associate Professor, North Carolina State University, and Director of the Privacy-Place.org.

back in the bottle' likely would be of limited value."[23] The FTC used this claim as the reason for completely ignoring said widespread use and availability and instead "believes that the central component of the solution is to reduce the demand for SSNs by minimizing their value to identity thieves."[24] In the same report, the FTC referred to SSNs as the "keys to the kingdom because an identity thief with a consumer's SSN may be able to use that information to convince a business that he is who he purports to be, allowing him to open new accounts, access existing accounts, or obtain other benefits in the consumer's name."[25]

This is a classic example of an inappropriate structure to combat identity theft. The FTC recognizes SSNs as the key component to identity theft, concludes the widespread use and availability of SSNs cannot be contained and thus recommends a solution of minimizing the value of SSNs. After reading (and rereading) this section, I had to walk away from it because it was impossible for me to believe the FTC could possibly reach such an idiotic conclusion in such an important report. Keep in mind this was not a conversation among staffers at the watercooler. When I returned to the report, I realized that I had not misread it. How does one go about decreasing the value of the keys to the kingdom? Just when you think it cannot get any worse: "This [decreas-

---

23   Transcript of SSN Workshop (Dec. 10, 2007) at 254-55 and Transcript of SSN Workshop (Dec. 11, 2007) at 126-27, Remarks of Tom Oscherwitz, Vice President of Government Affairs and Chief Privacy Officer, ID Analytics; Transcript of SSN Workshop (Dec. 11, 2007) at 155, Remarks of Fred Cate, Distinguished Professor and Director for Applied Cybersecurity Research, Indiana University, and Senior Policy Advisor, Center for Information Policy Leadership, Hunton & Williams.

24   "Security in Numbers *** - ** - *** SSNs and ID Theft." Federal Trade Commission Report. December 2008. p 6.

25   Ibid. p 3.

ing value of SSNs] could be achieved by encouraging or requiring entities that have consumer accounts that can be targeted by identity thieves to adopt more effective authentication procedures."[26] WHAT?!?! Tell me which accounts are not targets of identity thieves? If there is a loophole and value can be gained from stealing the identity, the thieves will steal your grandma's account at the local bingo parlor. And given the FTC's tremendous track record thus far in preventing identity theft, explain to me how they plan to successfully administer a program that encourages *more* effective authentication procedures?

This conclusion was made in lieu of another program that limited the transfers of SSNs; the FTC believed it to be too difficult to draft with sufficient precision.[27] What planet are these people from? The organization that is *assumed* lead-in-charge of preventing identity theft concludes that it is easier to regulate *every* authentication process than to draft legislation that limits the transfer of SSNs only for acceptable uses? It is this type of thinking that creates more bureaucracy, and increased bureaucracy creates more loopholes and opportunities for identity thieves. If I were reading this report aloud to a roomful of identity thieves, I would expect giggles and high fives since they know this is going to be a good business for a long time.

The purpose of this example is to illustrate the impossibility of creating a secure structure for SSNs as a national identifier; it simply was not designed for such a use. If it were not such an important issue, it would be comical to

---

26   "Security in Numbers *** - ** - *** SSNs and ID Theft." Federal Trade Commission Report. December 2008. p 6.

27   FTC Staff Summary, Transcript of SSN Workshop. December 10, 2007 at 156.

witness well-intentioned and intelligent people reach outrageous and counterintuitive solutions all because they are trying to pound a large square peg into a small round hole.

As previously mentioned, there are valid concerns regarding civil liberties and whether SSNs should be officially considered as a national ID (or whether a national identity system should even exist). We can continue to act as though the SSN is not a national identity scheme, but it is impossible to refute that it is often used in this manner and should receive commensurate attention and safeguards. There are relatively simple adjustments to the current system, such as random assignment of numbers, counterfeit-proof cards with biometrics and phasing out of previous versions, that would go a long way in securing the system. Also, since participation in the Social Security program is voluntary, it is not mandatory to have a number or card, and thus critics of an official national identity scheme need not be concerned.

I have gone into great detail explaining the Social Security system because SSNs truly are the *keys to the kingdom* for identity theft; thus, in order to correctly understand identity theft (and more importantly understand what can be done to minimize its likelihood), it is essential to understand the background. Many so-called experts and journalists miss this fundamental point and disseminate fallacious information, which further complicates this already complex topic. Without this knowledge, it is impossible to reach any useful conclusions or solutions. Now that we have firmly laid this foundation, we can pivot to the specifics of identity theft and consider its different forms, how the crime is commonly perpetrated and simple defense tactics.

 # Chapter 2

Identity Theft 101:
Knowing is Half the Battle

This chapter provides a comprehensive overview of identity theft, and the purpose is to give you a basic proficiency in identity theft concepts, landscape and terminology. It is easy to fill volumes with identity theft tactics, examples and statistics; however, this does little to help you prevent or recover from identity theft. Statistics and general information are considered, but let this chapter lend context to the overall crime. Let's start with the *definition of identity theft* according to the Federal Trade Commission:

> Identity theft occurs when someone uses your personally identifying information like your name, Social Security number, or credit card number, without your permission, to commit fraud or other crimes.[28]

It is important to note that it is technically impossible to have your identity stolen. Consider the concept of having your car stolen: you no longer have your car. With identity theft, you still have your identity, but someone else is *also* fraudulently using your identity.

---

28   "About Identity Theft." Federal Trade Commission. <http://www.ftc.gov/bcp/edu/microsites/idtheft/consumers/about-identity-theft.html>

A more accurate definition would clarify the crime with a few additional words: "…when someone uses or *intends to use* your or *fictional* personally identifying information…" Whether the criminal is successful with the crime or has utilized a real person's identification has no bearing on whether or not an identity has been compromised and/or stolen (the argument of creating an identity and considering this identity theft is discussed later in the chapter). If a robber holds up a bank at gunpoint, then he or she has committed a crime. Whether or not he or she actually is able to get away with the loot does not negate this fact. The same is true with identity theft, and this is defined in the Identity Theft Act.[29]

It is extremely important to make this clarification to include *intent* because this proves that everyone has had his or her identity stolen. The fact that there have been more records breached than total population supports this claim because the only reason to breach records is when the perpetrator *intends* to commit identity fraud. This fact is important for three primary reasons: 1) it provides a specific, definable and understandable illustration about the breadth of identity theft, 2) victims of identity theft are provided certain privileges under the law (this is discussed in greater detail later) and 3) it proves that it is impossible to prevent identity theft.

Take a moment to think and consider this: everyone has had his or her identity stolen and it is impossible to prevent. If you refuse to believe that your identity is at risk, then you render yourself a prime target for identity thieves.

---

29   Identity Theft Assumption and Deterrence Act of 1998 states, "…a means of identification of another person with the intent to commit, or to aid or abet, any unlawful activity that constitutes a violation of Federal law…" <http://www.ftc.gov/os/statutes/itada/itadact.htm>

Society needs to make a paradigm shift the way it considers identity theft from "it is possible that it will happen to me" to "it has *already* happened to me." You cannot prevent your identity information from being breached, as this has already happened.

While it makes sense to minimize the occurrences of identity theft, it is more important to diminish the value of the theft. Think of this hypothetical: If you understand that regardless of what you do your enemy is going to obtain a "gun," then you know that the bullets are what make the gun valuable (and are also the scarcer of the two resources). Then your primary focus becomes making certain your enemy cannot get the bullets to hurt you. Sure, you do not want to hand them the gun, but your most important task is preventing them from getting the ammunition. It's as simple as this: if they do not get the bullets, they cannot harm you. The same goes for identity theft. They may already have your information, but you still control whether you allow them to harm you with it.

I am often asked why I cannot prevent identity theft, and my answer is that the system does not allow it. I have a bank account, and I cannot force my bank to prevent my records from being stolen. I have a driver's license, and I cannot force the Department of Motor Vehicles to prevent my records from being stolen. I have an e-mail account, and I cannot force my e-mail provider to prevent my records from being stolen. Now you may begin to understand the limitations of the system.

The good news is that if you are well informed, then you have many opportunities to minimize the likelihood that you are negatively impacted by the theft. You may select to only work with a bank that has good security standards or an e-mail provider that does not require your SSN to open an account, etc. I estimate that greater than 95 percent of the pain associated with identity theft can be prevented by practicing simple and quick defense tactics.

Since the purpose of this book is not to get stuck in theoretical arguments regarding terminology, when I refer to identity theft *prevention*, I am referring to both preventing the occurrences of identity theft as well preventing thieves from achieving economic gain resulting from identity theft.

Forms of Identity Theft

There are many different forms of identity theft, but a vast majority of the overall attention is commonly placed on financial identity theft. Solely considering financial identity theft presents a significant risk to the average person since other forms of the theft can cause considerably more damage. It is generally agreed that the following are the five primary categories of identity theft:

1. Financial
2. Medical
3. Driver's License
4. Social Security
5. Criminal

FINANCIAL IDENTITY THEFT

This type of theft is when someone steals your identity to obtain loans, goods or services. This can mean utilizing credit card accounts in your name, purchasing merchandise, establishing utility accounts, obtaining mortgage loans or opening up bank accounts (to name a few). Unfortunately, this crime is so pervasive that many companies and individuals consider this as a cost of doing business.

You may think it's a minor inconvenience if your credit card company calls you and it is discovered that your account has been compromised. Most likely, the charges will be reversed, and you'll be issued a new card. However, if you have had multiple accounts fraudulently opened in your name, you will need to go through the very painful process of recovery, deal with unscrupulous collection agencies, repair your credit and/or deal with the feeling of powerlessness. This is often a life-changing event: it consumes a considerable amount of time, causes you aggravation and often has a significant negative economic and emotional impact on you and your family.

MEDICAL IDENTITY THEFT

This type of theft is where someone steals your identity to either obtain medical insurance in your name or use your current medical insurance policy to receive treatment or prescriptions. It is difficult to prevent and detect and can have deadly consequences. Imagine a situation where you are rushed to a hospital while unconscious. The emergency room doctor quickly reviews your medical record and administers a drug to which you are extremely allergic. If someone had previously used your identity to receive medical attention, he or she would have created a false medical record. That drug allergy would have not been present, and you could die from the allergic reaction to the medication.

Death is obviously the worst-case scenario, but the

following are also potential negative consequences of medical identity theft:

- False health insurance claims.

- False medical and pharmaceutical bills.

- Denial of health insurance claims or coverage.

- Denial of life insurance claims or coverage.

- Denial of employment based on false medical history.

- Time and expense correcting false patient and insurance records.

DRIVER'S LICENSE IDENTITY THEFT

This type of theft is where someone steals your identity and uses it during a traffic-related offense. This theft may occur because the perpetrator wants to avoid a ticket or because he or she is unable to obtain a license due to a DUI or other conviction. Similar to the other types of identity theft, it is often difficult to detect this form of theft. Oftentimes there is a minor event, such as an increase in insurance premiums, to indicate the theft; however, there are other more serious events like when a bench warrant is issued for arrest due to failure to appear, DUI/DWI charges or driving on a suspended license. The ultimate result can be facing time in jail, spending money to hire an attorney to restore your identity, taking time off of work for court appearances or even suffering public embarrassment. All of these scenarios are stressful and debilitating.

SOCIAL SECURITY IDENTITY THEFT

As the name implies, this theft occurs when someone steals

your Social Security number (SSN) and uses it obtain employment. While a compromised SSN may be used in order to commit other types of identity theft, it is only when it is used in order to obtain employment that is it considered *Social Security* identity theft. This type of theft is commonly used when illegal aliens attempt to acquire employment in the United States. A SSN that is validated by the Social Security Administration allows an illegal alien to "legally" work and also provides the employer legal protection. The SSN verification reports that the alien is using a valid SSN. This can happen because, as you remember, there is no biometric information with Social Security cards, so the employer can only rely on the SSN verification system.

The income earned by the Social Security identity thief is then reported to the IRS without any knowledge of the victim. The result can be a tax lien for failure to pay taxes on this income, which also can be sent to the credit reporting agencies and damage your credit rating. Other adverse consequences include denial of unemployment benefits (because the records indicate you are working) or denial of Social Security benefits such as Aid to Families with Dependent Children (because the records inappropriately inflate income).

CRIMINAL IDENTITY THEFT

This final type of identity theft is when someone steals your identity and fraudulently provides your information to a law enforcement officer during an investigation or upon arrest. Similar to driver's license identity theft, the innocent victim typically learns of the theft during a routine traffic stop or, worse, if there's a warrant and subsequently a raid is executed. In addition to the obvious legal implications, a victim may also be denied employment or terminated due to a fraudulent criminal record. It is also difficult to restore your records due to the disparate criminal record systems between cities, counties and the federal government and non-standardized procedures for clearing a wrongful criminal record. This often requires a significant time and monetary investment in the form of legal counsel to resolve.

All categories of identity theft are clear and present dangers for the average American citizen. Even more alarming are the *secondary categories,* which do not have as high of an incident rate as the primary categories but have effects that can be even more devastating. It is well known and documented that the terrorists from 9/11 utilized identity theft to execute many critical components of their plan. Also, narco-trafficking relies heavily on identity theft.

As we have expanded our knowledge foundation of identity theft by gaining an understanding of the various forms, we can now focus on the strategies and tactics.

 # Chapter 3

Identity Theft Strategies and Tactics

A *strategy* is an elaborate and systematic plan of action. For example, a common identity theft strategy is to steal electronic personally identifying data. *Tactics* are the specific methods utilized to execute the strategy. If the strategy is to steal electronic personally identifying data, then a viable tactic is to execute a data breach. Another viable tactic to execute this strategy is a phishing scam. Commonly there are multiple tactics utilized in executing a single strategy. All relate back to the overall mission: steal identities.

The old adage "the only constant is change" is particularly applicable to identity theft. An identity thief considers the industry much like an investor considers a business opportunity: What are my risks? What is my breakeven? What is my capital investment? What are worst-case, most-likely and best-case scenarios? Ultimately, what is my expected return on investment? Imagine you are the Original Equipment Manufacturer of one of the most valuable products ever and your capital investment and costs to produce are negligible. This depicts the identity theft industry with its astronomically disproportionate ratio of returns versus risk, costs and investment.

As we continue to become better educated as a society and create laws that make the crime more difficult to execute, this decreases their return on investment (ROI). However, decreasing ROI from 1000 percent to 950 percent is not going to cause them to exit the industry. To the contrary, the thieves recapitalize and develop more efficient strategies and tactics. This is their core competency, and they continue to refine their business model. Identity theft is considered the top crime concern for Americans, but how many resources do we dedicate to combat this crime? How much time do you devote on a daily basis to protect yourself? Do you have a daily defense plan that includes standard operating procedures such as verifying your anti-spyware software is updated, researching latest identity theft trends and news or verifying all personally identifying documentation is shredded prior to being placed in the trash?

The reality is identity theft is an afterthought or nuisance that the average American only deals with when he or she is forced to. In essence, we are fighting a well-funded, organized and educated team in our spare time with our ill-equipped junior varsity squad. With this understanding, it should come as no surprise that we are badly losing this battle.

Strategies

While the thieves' tactics are constantly changing and evolving, the general strategies fit into one of the following classifications:

1. Real Person Identity Theft

2. Synthetic Identity Theft

3. No Person Identity Theft

Real Person Identity Theft

This is the classification most commonly associated with identity theft. This occurs when an identity thief steals and/or assumes all components of your identity or of a *real person*. Everything from your name to your SSN to your date of birth is stolen. This is the version of the crime that is easiest to understand and detect, but as you will learn in the next two categories (and for this same reason), it also presents the least threat to society (albeit it is still a threat).

Synthetic Identity Theft

This occurs when a thief utilizes some real components of your identity and mixes them with fictitious components to create a new *synthetic* identity. For example, a thief may use your name and Social Security number, but utilize his or her date of birth and address. The challenges of synthetic identity theft are that it is very pervasive (ID Analytics estimates it accounts for approximately 90 percent of the identity theft incidents[30]), and it is extremely difficult to detect. If executed effectively, the synthetic identity and resulting financial activity does not appear immediately (or ever) on the real person's credit report. So, even if you practice defense strategies discussed later in this book, you still may not be able to prevent or even detect synthetic identity theft. It is a rather complicated topic, and for our purposes, it is important to have a general understanding of this crime.

---

30   "ID Analytics announces new data analysis findings: Synthetic Identity Fraud poses new challenges." ID Analytics. February 9, 2005.   <http://www.idanalytics.com/news-and-events/news-releases/2005/2-9-2005.php>

No Person Identity Theft

This occurs when a thief creates a completely fictitious identity (with no intentional components of a real person's identity). This is a new concept or classification that I am introducing. It is commonly believed that creating a fictitious identity is not considered identity theft. If the fictitious identity is utilized in a crime, then it is considered identity fraud but not identity theft. In fact, in 2009 the Supreme Court case *Flores-Figueroa v. U.S.* 08-108 had a unanimous decision stating that if a person does not knowingly use another person's identity to commit fraud that it is not considered identity theft.

It appears the main defense is grounded in jurisprudence and the common law definition of theft as the knowledge that the stolen property belongs to someone else.[31] While I am attempting not to digress into legal babble, it is necessary to present the following argument to support my final conclusion that identity fraud executed without any component of a real person's identity, knowingly or unknowingly, is identity theft.

If one is to steal a stapler from a business, then this is considered theft (think of the disruption "my stapler" caused in the movie *Office Space!*). This allows us to broaden our definition of *someone* beyond a specific person. If this stapler is stolen from the common area in an office complex, then the criminal may not *know* to whom specifically it belongs, but he or she knows or *should reasonably know* that it belongs to someone (and most likely one of the companies in the office complex). Thus, if someone steals a stapler

---

31   Kristina Moore. "Opinion Recap for *Flores-Figueroa v. U.S.*" <http://www.scotusblog.com/?p=9428>

from the common office area, it is considered "theft."

Identities are part of the social fabric and infrastructure of society. Each person is inalienably allowed one identity within this structure, and this is a truth self-evident and even *more unalienable* than the rights of life, liberty and pursuit of happiness. Thus, to steal a component or the entirety of another's identity is a theft against both the individual *and* society as a whole. Both are victims.

To create an entirely fictitious identity is a crime of identity theft *only against society*. In this sense, the aggrieved *someone* is society or the aggregate of the individuals. Whether the victim is an individual, a group or society, the criminal act of identity theft has been perpetrated.

The identity theft strategies are Real Person, Synthetic and No Person, and each presents challenges to individuals and society. The strategies are elaborate and systematic plans of action, and next we consider methods utilized to execute these strategies: the tactics.

Tactics

The only constant is change. It is worth repeating because thieves constantly change, adapt and continue to better the skills of their trade. If we do not accept this fact, then we will continue to lose this war. For every new law or detection system, there are special operations teams of thieves discovering loopholes or, even worse, they are determining new, improved tactics that otherwise would not have existed, like a mutated, stronger strain of a virus. For example, the false sense of security as well as the misunderstood service provided by credit monitoring services (these are detection and *not* prevention services, and the crucially important difference is discussed later in the book) often leads consumers to misdirect invaluable resources away from sound identity theft prevention practices. The thieves exploit this opportunity.

As we continue to progress through the electronic age, identity theft skills are becoming increasingly sophisticated. While old-fashioned methods such as stealing personally identifying information from the trash still exist, the thieves can attain a much better ROI through advanced strategies that include stealing in bulk through endeavors such as mass data breaches with millions of personally sensitive data records stolen.

The primary tool necessary for the thieves to execute their crime is attaining personally identifying information (PII). This is information that uniquely identifies an individual. Some PII, such as names, are shared by many and are widely available; so, they are not quite as valuable as other PII such as Social Security numbers, which are a purely unique identifier (maximum one SSN per individual, at least legally). Other examples of PII include age, date of birth, address, fingerprints, face, driver's license number, sex and gender.

The more accurate PII a thief can attain, the better the likelihood of stealing an identity. For example, if a thief only has a person's name, then it is probably very difficult to access this person's checking account. However, if the thief has the person's name, SSN, address, date of birth, mother's maiden name, then it is likely that a knowledgeable thief can access this account (and many more accounts).

The following are examples and explanations of the most common identity theft tactics, and the goal for each tactic is to acquire PII. Because the tactics are constantly changing, this should not be considered a complete list. It is essential to continually self-educate to stay current on the most recent tactics as well as new defense strategies. There are easy-to-understand sites such as TheIDChannel.com that aggregate the latest news, events, trends and tactics of identity thieves. Also, the Identity Ambassador Commission (IdentityAmbassador.org) distributes a free monthly newsletter that serves a similar purpose. The Identity Theft Resource Center (IDTheftCenter.org) provides victim and consumer support as well as public education.

PHYSICALLY STEALING DOCUMENTS

Dumpster Diving

Since I already referenced this tactic, I thought I would start with it. This term refers to rummaging through trash to retrieve items of value. "Diving" derives from the image of going head first into a commercial dumpster thus, *dumpster diving*. Things of value include furniture, equipment or even televisions, but in relationship to identity theft, the diver is seeking documents with important personally identifying information (PII). This consists of preapproved offers of credit, credit receipts, letters from the government including a SSN, notices from credit bureaus or bills (to name a few). While this tactic is a little old-fashioned in the electronic age, it is still widely used and produces great results for the thieves.

Purse or Wallet Snatching

A substantial percentage of identity theft results from purse or wallet snatching. Until relatively recently, most were taught to carry his or her Social Security card with them (in a wallet or purse). So, in addition to the currency in a wallet or purse, the thief has a veritable gold mine with the SS card, credit cards, ATM cards, medical insurance card, checkbook and a driver's license. Some have such elaborate systems that they can drain your accounts mere minutes after the theft. In fact, Anna Bernanke, wife of the chairman of the Federal Reserve, had her purse snatched off the back of her chair at a Starbucks in Washington, D.C. According to court records, on August 7, 2008, she had her driver's license, SS card, four credit cards and a book of checks from the joint account at Wachovia complete with the bank account number, address and telephone number printed on each check stolen. The thief was part of a sophisticated crime ring and within days checks from their joint account were being cashed. This example proves that even the Federal Reserve chairman can have his identity stolen. Nobody is immune to this crime.

Mail Theft

This is a cleaner and more efficient version of dumpster diving as the thieves do not need to deal with rotten tomatoes to collect the desired documents. While thieves are generally seeking the same information, such as credit card applications, they have an additional benefit of sifting through outgoing mail that includes valuable bills that you are paying by check or credit card. This tactic is more commonplace at apartment buildings or housing complexes. Here there are several households and the mail is combined in one location. Without single ownership of the mailbox, the thief's intent is not as obvious.

Check Fraud

Printing fake checks, stealing checks (the Bernankes'),

ordering checks in someone else's name or tampering with real checks is still a common tactic of thieves. Because identity theft has transitioned into the electronic age and most only minimally consider this tactic (if at all), it continues to be a popular method with increasing losses. This can be more dangerous than credit card or ATM fraud since the perpetrator can access cash and does not require a PIN.

Data Breach

This is when secure electronic records are stolen or compromised. This is typically done in large quantities. Electronic data does not require near the space as documents of physical data. For example, in 2007 hackers breached 45.7 million data records from T.J. Maxx credit and debit card customers. Also, as discussed previously, according to the Privacy Rights Clearinghouse, there have been nearly two times *reported* records breached since 2005 than the entire U.S. population! Keep in mind, data breaches do not include any improper or reckless actions by the consumers and they have no control over this type of theft.

Internal Theft

This occurs when identities are stolen by employees or clients of companies that retain sensitive data, such as loan offices or credit agencies. The most well-known example of this type of theft happened in 2005 to ChoicePoint, which is one of the largest data aggregators. Identity thieves set up fake businesses and purchased the personal information of 163,000 consumers. Even though most have never heard of ChoicePoint or have ever provided permission to obtain personal information—it compiles, stores and sells this personal information. People's most sensitive data was compromised by a company that they did not even know and certainly did not authorize to collect their information. This is another example of how your identity is stolen through a company and service of which you have absolutely no control.

Data Theft

Data theft differs from internal theft since these data breaches are not conducted by employees or clients. These are external agents like hackers who are able to steal sensitive personal data. PriceWaterhouseCoopers conducted ethical hacking tests and was successful nearly 90 percent of the time in gaining access to highly sensitive information.[32] With this type of success rate, it should come as no surprise that there have been more than 500 million documented data breaches since 2005.

Mail Redirection

This occurs when the thief contacts the USPS or creditors to have your personal mail sent to another address. This is particularly dangerous; reviewing mail and accounts is often one of the best methods for detecting when accounts are compromised. Without this critical correspondence, unknowing consumers often do not realize the fraudulent activity. Additionally, the thief is then directly receiving significant PII, eliminating the need for dumpster diving.

---

32   "10 Minutes on Data and Identity Theft." PriceWaterhouseC-oopers. October 2008. p 1.

The change of address process with the USPS is completed online with a basic identity validation via a $1 charge to your credit card.[33] Or it can be done by completing and submitting a USPS Form 3575, which has *no* identity validation. In order to redirect mail in the United Kingdom, the system requires submission of two *original* identity documents, one of which must be a government-issued photo ID. The U.K. understands the significance of this tactic and has applied the appropriate safeguards.

Child Identity Theft

This tactic is gaining the most traction in identity theft circles because one of the most important components, the time from theft to detection, is in their favor. In other words, the longer the thief is able to operate undetected, the greater the returns. There are many contributory factors for this trend, and the most important is that parents do not realize their children are an at-risk group. Credit issuers do not have a way to verify the age of an applicant, and this issue is compounded by the fact that most applications are not completed face-to-face, thus no proof of identity, such as a driver's license, is required. Furthermore, Credit Reporting Agencies (CRAs) establish the age of customers at the time of their first credit application. So, if the child's identity is stolen and the first credit application indicates the age of 25, then this is established with the CRAs until proven otherwise. If this theft occurs when the child is five, then this commonly can take 10 plus years before

---

33   "Change your address online." United States Postal Service. <https://moversguide.usps.com/icoa/flow.do?_flowExecutionKey=_ cF107264C-32D3-6BBD-6446-DF9124465BD5_kD64DF310-F82C-083B- 603A-D3566CA0CD1D>

anyone even realizes the identity was stolen. The parents were not practicing any defense or detection tactics for their children. In fact, many have been denied the ability to attend college because their identity was stolen as a child and the resulting bad credit prevented them from receiving financial aid to attend.

Deceased Identity Theft

Stealing the identity of the deceased is a popular tactic for one obvious reason: the victim rarely complains! But, there are some not-so-obvious logistical reasons, which make this an even more attractive tactic. First, it is relatively easy to learn about deceased individuals from items including obituaries, stolen death certificates or even from the Social Security Death Index file. Once an individual is deceased, it takes time for financial institutions to receive the often incomplete and erroneous SS Death Master File and update their records. If an authorized representative does not contact creditors or the CRAs to close accounts, then these accounts often remain open for up to 10 years. This tactic will remain popular until this type of theft is made more difficult and the average time between theft and detection significantly decreases.

Computer Spyware

This is software installed on your computer without your consent (and normally without your knowledge) that monitors or controls your computer use. The thief is able to access everything you do online including usernames and passwords, which allows him or her access to your personal information and accounts (i.e., online banking). This tactic is more valuable to thieves when there are several users of a single machine, such as at a coffee shop or library. There is an example in New York where the thief Juju Jiang covertly installed spyware that logged keystrokes in at least a dozen Kinko's stores. With this spyware he captured more than 400 usernames and passwords that he used to access, and even open up, bank accounts online!

Phishing

This tactic involves attaining PII and/or sensitive information, such as usernames and passwords by posing as a valid entity like a bank representative. This is carried out by e-mail, instant messaging or telephone. *Pharming* is a common example of phishing whereby the victim is directed to a bogus website that has a look and feel that's almost identical to the legitimate site. This makes the target feel comfortable providing secure information.

In 2003 there was a phishing/pharming scam that had e-mails sent supposedly from eBay claiming the user account was about to be suspended unless he or she clicked on the provided link and updated his or her credit card information. Of course, the link brought the user to the fraudster's website, which had an identical look and feel to eBay, thus making the user comfortable providing the sensitive credit card information.

In the case of phone phishing (aka *pretexting*), the thief may call posing as a bank representative indicating that you have been a victim of identity theft and subsequently request that you verify information to confirm your identity. The catch is that you are only confirming information the thief already knows, like your name and address, and then you provide unknown, valuable information, such as your account number or SSN. The thief is actually using identity theft as a cover to commit identity theft!

Shoulder Surfing

This low-technology approach involves the thief accumulating PII while you conduct personal business in a public setting. The thief simply listens intently to phone conversations, peers over your shoulder as you enter information to the ATM or watches as you write down or enter information into your computer.

Skimming

This process entails utilizing a device similar to a credit card reader to illegally collect data from the magnetic strip of a credit or debit card and then transfers it to a blank card's magnetic strip. This cloned card can then be used and read by true credit card machines or to process transactions online as though it is the original card. This commonly takes place at restaurants. The thief or server takes the card to settle the bill and additionally copies the card to the skimming device, which fits into his or her pocket. It only takes a couple seconds to complete, though the thief also needs to physically write down the security code not contained in the data in the magnetic strip. These devices can easily be purchased online for approximately $50.

This is also becoming increasingly common at ATM machines and gas stations. The device goes directly over the normal card reading slot and the information is sent wirelessly to the thief or even transmitted via a text message to a cell phone. Either a hidden camera or a false keypad used as a logging device works with the skimmer to attain the information not contained in the magnetic strip, such as PIN or zip code.

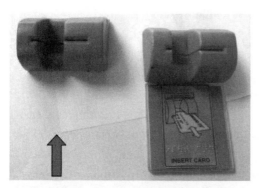

The real card reader slot. The capture device

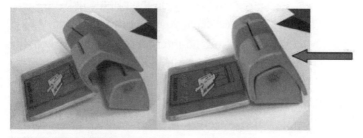

The side cut out is not visible when on the ATM.

ATM Skimming Device[34]

Wireless Hacking

This tactic involves accessing and hacking wireless networks. Once the network is compromised, the thieves use programs to access card and PIN numbers, which are sent to servers and often end up for sale online. *Wardriving* is

---

34   "ATM   Skimming   Device."   <http://krebsonsecurity. com/2010/01/would-you-have-spotted-the-fraud/>

a form of wireless hacking that involves thieves driving around with a laptop and trying to access wireless networks within range of the car. We discussed earlier the 45.7 million credit and debit card numbers breached at T.J. Maxx, and this was made possible by wireless hacking. Investigators believe the hackers pointed a telescope-shaped antenna towards a store in St. Paul, MN, and used a laptop to decode data streaming through the air between hand-held price-checking devices and the store's computers. This allowed them to hack into the central database in Framingham, MA, to repeatedly steal information about the customers over an 18-month period without detection. Some of the internal investigations claim that as many as 200 million card numbers were compromised and that the wireless network had less security than many people have on their home networks.[35]

Whether you are eating at your favorite restaurant, talking on the phone, surfing the Internet or playing basketball at the gym (in other words, almost anything you are doing), identity thieves have a tactic to exploit your action or lack of action. That is the bad news. The good news is there are many simple defense tactics that eliminate a vast majority of the theft incidents. As with most components of this misunderstood and inaccurately reported crime, effective defense strategies are poorly developed and communicated, thus exacerbating the negative effects of the crime. Before we discuss specific defense tactics, it is necessary to define the difference between defense strategies.

---

35   Michael Gough. "How Wi-Fi networks are hacked and how to assess Wi-Fi networks." Wireless Hacking & Assessment. March 2, 2010. p 40.

 **Chapter 4**

Identity Theft Defense Strategies and Tactics: Prevention

There are three primary defense strategies that are often misrepresented or lumped all together. An effective overall defense plan requires an accurate understanding of each of the three main strategies: prevention, detection and recovery.

Prevention

Consider the following question: would you rather *prevent* identity theft or *detect* and *recover* from it? The same question considered in a different context: would you rather place a lock on your door to prevent a thief from stealing your jewels or notice they have been stolen and go through the process of filing reports with the police, insurance company, etc., to recover from the theft? The obvious choice is *prevent*.

One ounce of prevention is worth a pound of cure.

Unfortunately, most do not invest in the one ounce of prevention and thus are left with the one pound of cure. By definition, this strategy entails tactics that *avoid* identity theft all together. A majority of people do not understand *viable* prevention tactics, nor do they understand the minimal resource requirement (time or monetary) of these tactics. Thus, they are left with no (or minimal) prevention tactics or they practice misguided tactics that often create a false reality of protection. Since this is by far the most preferred strategy, we dedicate a vast majority of our attention to this method.

Detection

Similar to the lock on the door, no prevention tactic (or combination thereof) 100 percent guarantees the identity will not be stolen. It may stop 90 percent or more of the thieves but not all of them, especially the sophisticated thieves. As such, it is important to also practice sound *detection* tactics. Additionally, you need to understand which tactics are *preventive* versus *detective*. Understanding that consumers prefer preventing theft, many companies erroneously or deceptively market their detection services as "preventive." We will consider and discuss this unethical marketing in greater detail, but the important takeaway at this point is to understand that many companies (and companies that you would expect to be on *your* side) do not always have your best interests in mind.

Recovery

There are various types of recovery that require different levels of understanding of the system and the law. If your credit card was compromised, recovery may be as simple as a call to your credit card company. However, if someone commits crimes with your identity, then recovery may require a vast amount of resources and legal help to restore your identity, with the caveat that it may never fully be restored. For our purposes, recovery is the act (or acts) you must take to restore your stolen identity.

PREVENTION TACTICS

We have determined that most prefer to prevent pain instead of detect and recover from it. We have also determined that many products are mischaracterized as prevention when they are truly detection or recovery. So what are the most effective identity theft prevention tactics? The most important prevention tactic is to *pay attention*. Sure, we will discuss a few advanced tactics, but most of the following advice simply suggests a combination of paying attention and knowing how to act in certain situations. There are three common themes of all of these prevention tactics: 1) they are not complicated, 2) very little time is required and 3) they cost little or nothing.

Remember that as thieves' tactics are always changing so too are the prevention tactics. Even if you do not commit all of these tactics to memory, if you understand and practice the basic premise of *pay attention to indicators* and *execute common-sense practices*, then more than 99 percent of the identity theft incidences resulting in harm are avoided.

In today's society, sharing personally identifying information (PII) is necessary to function. Since this same PII represents the tool to the thieves' craft, the challenge is to make certain only the authorized party(s) has access to PII at the appropriate time(s). This seems easy enough! It becomes a tad bit more complicated considering that you do not always have control of who accesses your PII, and thieves are always scheming for ways to trick you into divulging this invaluable information.

Volumes can be dedicated to all of the possible prevention tactics. Instead of giving you information overload and to maximize the usefulness of this section, I have divided the tactics into two main categories: Quick Hits and Deep Dives.

The Quick Hits are tactics that are extremely simple and *quick* to employ. The Deep Dives are either a little more complicated or more effective and require further or *deeper* consideration. As with everything in this book, these tactics should be considered a starting point. If you want more information, simply enter the term into a search engine and you will receive mountains of information. As always, be careful. There is a vast amount of misinformation out there. However, once you have completed this book, you should be amply prepared to discern between *good* and *bad* information or sources.

Quick Hits

- Do not carry your Social Security card, birth certificate or passport unless it is required for a specific purpose.

- Do not carry extra credit cards.

- *Immediately* report to the proper institution lost or theft of any of the following (or other documents carrying valuable PII): credit card, Social Security card, driver's license, checkbook and health insurance card.

- Never use your driver's license as a form of collateral or security deposit (e.g., when automobile shopping).

- Contact your local DMV to request the "verify ID" option (states which have this option requires officers and licensing agents to request two forms of identity for validation).

- Do not click on links in any e-mails you receive from financial institutions *even if you know it is your financial institution.* Instead, go to the institution's website and login.

- Do not provide any information over the phone to any financial institution *even if you know it is your financial institution.* Instead, call back a number that can be verified (i.e., telephone number on the back of your credit card).

- Install virus and spyware detection software and keep them updated.

- Install a lockable mailbox at your residence.

- Take credit card receipts with you and *never* throw them in a public trash container.

- Do not place your Social Security number on job applications.

- *Never* leave your purse or wallet unattended anywhere including your locked car (and secure personal information, including medical statement of benefits, in your own home).

- Destroy all checks immediately after closing a checking account.

- Do not have the bank send new checks to your house. Instead, pick them up at the bank.

- Reconcile your check and credit card statements within a maximum of two weeks.

- Limit the number of credit and ATM cards you have. Cancel any unnecessary/inactive accounts.

- Never give your credit card, bank or Social Security number to anyone if you did not initiate the call.

- Do not write and do not allow your financial institution to print your SSN on your checks.

- Shred everything that has PII including credit, ATM, debit receipts, pre-approved offers for credit, bank statements, loan statements, medical statements or bills and utility bills before discarding.

- Verify subscription and utility bills to make certain they belong to you.

- Memorize your PINs and passwords so you do not need to write them down. Be aware of your surroundings when entering or providing these PINs or passwords.

- Do not provide ANY information to telemarketers.

- Do not open e-mails from people you do not know.

- Install a firewall to protect your home network.

- Do not access private information (i.e., online bank accounts) when utilizing public connections (i.e., a library or Starbucks).

- If using peer-to-peer (P2P) software, use a different computer to share files versus the computer that has sensitive PII.

- Turn off your computer when not in use.

- When shopping online, check the authenticity of websites and make certain they belong to a seal-of-approval program that abide by privacy-related rules.

- Write checks with gel pens so the ink will permeate the fibers.

- Do not download files from the Internet unless you have verified the source.

- Destroy the hard drive from your computer and photocopier if you are disposing it. Do not just erase the drive—physically remove and destroy it.

- On blogs or social networking sites, do not:

  o indicate when you are leaving on holiday.

  o make your full name (or children's names) public (use nicknames if possible).

  o post your address, phone number, driver's license number, SSN or student number.

Deep Dives

Place a fraud alert on your credit report every 90 days.

You have the right to request nationwide credit reporting agencies to place "fraud alerts" in your file to let potential creditors know that you may be a victim of identity theft. This alert requires creditors (when applying for new credit or increasing credit limit) to go through an extra verification layer to make certain it is really you who has made the credit request. Per the Fair Credit Reporting Act: the user (creditor) must utilize reasonable policies and procedures to form a reasonable belief that the user (creditor) knows the identity of the person making the request. Normally (although not required), the creditor contacts you at the phone number that you designate to verify you and only you have instigated the action.

In this book, we considered and concluded that everyone is a victim of identity theft; thus, everyone has the right to place fraud alerts on their reports. The alerts last 90 days; so, to continue this invaluable service, you must reset the alerts every 90 days. The alerts are free of charge and can be set with the companies through the following contact info:

Equifax: 1.877.576.5734; www.alerts.equifax.com
Experian: 1.888.397.3742; www.experian.com/fraud
TransUnion: 1.800.680.7289; www.transunion.com

Imagine the reduction in identity theft by simply requiring that credit card companies verify your identity when opening or increasing the limits on accounts! While this does not stop all identity theft and all of its various forms (no tactic does), it is my opinion that this is *by far* the best defense tactic.

Opt out of prescreened offers of credit or insurance.

Many creditors and insurance companies purchase your information from the credit reporting agencies to solicit you because your credit report indicates you meet their criteria. These offers often have considerable PII that ends up in your mailbox or trash (and are also a considerable annoyance and waste). You can cut the snake off at the head by opting out of these offers. If you opt out over the Internet or phone, it lasts for five years (you can always opt back in).

www.optoutprescreen.com

888.5.OPTOUT (678688)

To be fair and balanced, the credit reporting agencies (with an obvious profit motive) do contend that pre-screened offers of credit provide consumers with product choices, the ability to take advantage of offers that may not be available to the general public and comparison shop. It is your decision, but based on my personal opinion and an unscientific survey of friends and family, nearly all would rather bypass the so-called benefits to diminish the likelihood of identity theft (and rid themselves of needless trash).

Register your phone numbers with the National Do Not Call Registry.

This service prevents telemarketers from soliciting you at your registered number. It does not prevent companies with which you have a relationship from contacting and/ or soliciting you (e.g., you have a Bank of America checking account, and they call you to offer a Bank of America credit card). It is a common misnomer that companies may not solicit you at your mobile number. The reality is that it is legal to telemarket cell phones, but it is illegal to use automatic dialers (which is the industry norm). Either way, the registry accepts both landlines and cell numbers, so they cannot solicit you at either number if they are registered. The telemarketers must comply with your request once your number has been registered for 31 days.

www.donotcall.gov

1.888.382.1222

If you register through the website, you will receive a confirmation e-mail with instructions to finalize the process (it is required you have an e-mail address if you want to register via the website). If you register through the toll-free number, it is required that you call from the phone number for which you are registering. Similar to the reasons for opt out of prescreened offers, many scams are originated via the phone. The fewer calls you receive from unknown sources, the lower the likelihood that you are victim of one of these scams (it also reduces the annoying phone calls received during dinner!).

Secure your Social Security Number on your credit report.

As most are well aware, credit reports end up all over the place and in many places you would not authorize if you had the control. If you doubt me, just go into an auto dealership's finance office and view how many files are sitting around virtually unattended. A full credit report with all information is nirvana for identity thieves, and the most important component is the SSN. No SSN equals decreased value. Few know that you have a right to have the first five numbers of your Social Security number re- moved from your reports (in the "Disclosures to Consum- ers"), yielding only the last four (which also happen to be the least predictable). When requesting your credit report, simply request to have the first five digits of your Social Security Number masked.

Equifax
P.O. Box 740256
Atlanta, GA 30374

Experian
P.O. Box 9554
Allen, TX 75013

TransUnion
P.O. Box 6790
Fullerton, CA 92834

Author's Note: As I've noted earlier, I am also the founder of an identity theft prevention company, IDCuffs.com, and the first four Deep Dive components are part of the service offered. I believe the best way to combat identity theft is to provide as much free information as possible, so this is why I provide you a detailed outline of some of the most important components to my company. These are components that you should insist upon if you are going to engage any identity theft prevention *service. While IDCuffs.com certainly has additional benefits, these services should be considered a convenience and not proprietary knowledge. For example, if you decide the risk of forgetting to reset the fraud alert outweighs the minimal monthly convenience fee, then you are a good candidate for this service. I believe in complete transparency and you, as the consumer, should make an informed purchasing decision. Whether you purchase my service or not, my primary concern is that the chances of you experiencing identity theft are minimized. If you do want to purchase the service with a special discount, go to:*

https://www.idcuffs.com/signup
promo code: Handbook

Request that financial institutions place an extra security protection on your accounts.

This is a password (separate from the PIN) that is required to make any changes to the accounts such as changing mailing address, increasing available credit or requesting the setup of new accounts. Most financial institutions offer this service. Often thieves access your account, change the mailing address (so you do not immediately recognize the theft), increase your limit, drain the account and then move on to the next before you have a chance to notice and take effective action. This step substantially reduces the likelihood of this outcome. It is simple, free and provides tremendous value.

Be extra careful on social networking sites.

This could have been a Quick Hit, but with the recent and rapid explosion of users as well as the serious identity theft implications, it warrants a Deep Dive. A study by *Consumer Reports* indicates that "52 percent of adult users of social networks such as Facebook and MySpace have posted risky personal information online."[36] In other words, over half the social network users are simply donating their identities to the thieves. Aside from an obvious prevention tactic such as creating a strong, unique pass-

---

36   "Social Network Users Post Risky Infromation." *Consumer Reports*. <http://blogs.consumerreports.org/electronics/2010/05/social-networks-facebook-risks-privacy-risky-behavior-consumer-reports-survey-findings-online-threats-state-of-the-net-report.html>

word, here are social network-specific tactics:

1. Set proper privacy controls. You have the ability to limit access to friends, friends of friends or nobody. Do not allow unknown people (and this includes friends of friends because you can't guarantee that they practice good social networking protocol) have access to your personal information such as your birth date, family info or photos.

2. Only accept friends that you really know and trust. This may seem self-evident, but once you open yourself up, then your "friend" has access to your information and posts as well as potentially your friends' information and posts.

3. Limit the amount and type of personal information provided. You would not freely provide a stranger at the grocery store your full name, address, date of birth, etc. So, why provide it to someone (or everyone) who you do not even have the courtesy of meeting face-to-face? For example, consider only having your month and year of your birthday (or no birthday at all) listed in your profile. It also does not make sense to list your phone number or address because if anybody really needs this contact information, they can simply send you a note to request it and then it's up to you to share it or not.

4. Do not allow children to use social networks un-supervised. If it is difficult for adults to learn and utilize proper safety protocol, then all bets are off

when it comes to children. The vast amounts of valuable information children possess and the ease of which skilled criminals can convince children to divulge this information is extremely dangerous (and not just from an identity theft perspective). While it may be impossible to fully monitor your teenager's use, educate and inform them of the dangers and common-sense practices of using social networking sites.

5. Do not create a profile with a child's name or post it in a caption. As previously discussed, all an identity thief requires from a child is a name and SSN to get started. Age and address is established with the credit reporting agencies at the time of the first credit application. We also discussed the ease of predicting recently assigned SSNs. Displaying your children's name as well as posting their birthday and birthplace (two more key pieces for predicting SSNs), in the public domain provides an excellent target for thieves. Make certain you also request friends to remove tags or captions including your children's names.

Social networking sites can be fun and beneficial, but like everything else, you need to understand basic defense tactics to ensure continuous enjoyment.

If you faithfully practice the Deep Dive tactics and generally abide by the Quick Hit tactics, then you are comparable to an armored tank. It does not mean that you are impenetrable, but you are in much better shape than the person next to you hiding behind a few thin bushes. In addition to adopting these tactics, you should continue to self-educate and study identity theft. At this point, I must recommend and reiterate two free and easy-to-use services I created for the sole purpose of educating the consumer.

TheIDChannel.com is a central, dependable, comprehensive and timely resource of industry news and information. While it encourages community interaction and participation, all user-submitted information is vetted to guarantee accuracy and relevancy. A quick perusal of the latest news, videos and blogs provides the average consumer invaluable insight into identity theft information, trends and defense tactics.

The Identity Ambassador Commission (IdentityAmbassador.org) was designed to reverse the alarming trend of identity theft by providing education and training. Much of the information contained in this book is also contained in the training and testing for the Certified Identity Expert designation. The Commission disseminates a complimentary monthly newsletter that aggregates the most important identity theft news and information.

Unfortunately, due the asymmetric nature of identity theft, even the best tactics and defense fortifications cannot prevent all attacks against your identity. Even though it is common sense to devote far more attention and resources to *prevention*, a comprehensive overall strategy requires a good understanding of *detection* tactics, which are outlined in the next chapter.

Chapter 5

Identity Theft Defense Strategies and Tactics: Detection

Simply stated: if you have become a victim of identity theft, then you'd want to know about it as soon as possible. The longer the crime persists without detection, the more pain it causes. In this chapter, we consider the most effective detection tactics.

All of the Quick Hits are indicators that your identity has been compromised and are typically realized in coordination with another life event such as purchasing a car. The Deep Dives are specific processes designed with a singular purpose of detecting identity theft.

Quick Hits

- Bills do not arrive as expected.

- Unexpected credit card statements.

- Denial of credit for no apparent reason.

- Approval of credit at terms not commensurate with risk profile.

- Calls or letters about purchases you did not make.

- Unauthorized charges or accounts on credit report.

- You try to make a legitimate insurance claim and

your health plan states that you have reached your limit on benefits.

- You are denied insurance for a condition you do not have.

Deep Dives

Review your credit report from all three credit bureaus for unauthorized activity.

You need to periodically obtain and review your credit report. You can receive one free copy of your credit report each year from each bureau via www.annualcreditreport.com (this is also included as part of the service of IDCuffs.com). An argument persists within the identity theft industry of "how often" it is necessary to review your credit report. The credit reporting agencies (and their resellers) attempt to convince unknowing consumers that they should continuously monitor their credit. This idea works well in a vacuum tube where all elements are controlled, but not so well when you consider real world and dynamic applications. Here are some of the shortcomings:

1. False sense of security. This service points out changes to your credit file but only *after the changes were made*. Combine this with deceptive marketing of the bureaus that pitch monitoring as prevention and it creates a false sense of security. You cannot undo what is already done, and monitoring only informs you of what has already been done. Many consumers with monitoring services shortchange the more important prevention components because they wrongly assume monitoring is prevention.

2. Information overload. The alerts are frequently incorrect but not consequential. After receiving regular doses of meaningless information, the consumer reaches information saturation and begins to disregard alerts altogether (yet still believes the service protects him or her). If the monitoring service reports all three bureaus, then changes that occur on all three bureaus means the consumer receives the same alert three times.

3. Some of the services only provide monitoring of one bureau. On the flip side, if the fraud occurs with either of the other bureaus, then you are not even notified.

4. The service does not even detect identity theft. It is the consumer's responsibility to reconcile the alerts (which he or she may not be paying attention to) with the facts to determine if the identity has been compromised.

At the end of the day, the credit reporting agencies are going to brand, market and advertise this service with everything they have because monitoring is a cash cow for them. It is a completely automated service so all of the revenue (less the branding, marketing and advertising) is pure profit. They are not actually "doing" anything. They do not really care if your identity is stolen because they are not even going to assist you. They will refer you to the FTC, original creditors and anybody else so that they can do as little as possible. The average consumer is duped into a product that does not protect his or her identity and most likely will not even detect identity theft when it occurs.

I would never advise against any product or service that

assists the overall strategy of combating identity theft. In the case of monitoring, it is my opinion that a close review of the free yearly reports (plus any reviews if you apply for credit and receive the report) is sufficient when done in conjunction with comprehensive prevention tactics. So, if you understand what service you are getting and not sacrificing prevention, then by all means go for it. However, if you are solely depending on monitoring as a prevention tactic, then you are playing *identity roulette*.

When reviewing yearly credit reports, it is important to understand the credit report and what to look for:

1. Is there any incorrect personal information? Wrong address(es), name(s), SSN(s) or date of birth(s)?

2. Do all the credit accounts belong to you?

3. Are there unpaid debts and/or collections that do not belong to you?

4. Is there information in public records (bankruptcies, judgments or tax liens) that does not belong to you?

If there is incorrect information, then you will need to execute the appropriate tactics based on the type of identity theft (i.e., a medical collection may indicate medical identity theft) discussed in the *recovery* chapter.

MEDICAL

In addition to reviewing your credit report for erroneous medical-related accounts, the following are specific tactics for detecting medical identity theft. The most useful tactic is to review your Explanation of Benefits (EOB) statement your health plan sends after each treatment. Specifically review for accuracy the name of the provider, date of service and service provided. You should also request a summary each year for benefits paid from medical insurers for the same reasons. Lastly, the Health Insurance Portability and Accountability Act (HIPAA) Privacy Rule provides you the right to your records from the insurers and medical providers. Unlike credit reports, there is not a central database for this information. So, you should request and review these records individually for inaccuracies before seeking additional medical care. If there are discrepancies with any of these records, refer to the next chapter.

DRIVER'S LICENSE

A review of your credit report most likely will not indicate driver's license identity theft, so it is necessary to obtain a copy of your driving record and check for erroneous information. You can learn the process of ordering your driving record from DMV.org, which is not part of any DMV but provides beneficial information regarding DMVs.[37] Some states allow you to order online, while others require notarized application forms. All states allow you to request the driving record at the local DMV office. There is normally a nominal fee involved with the request (approximately $5–$10). If there are any discrepancies with the driving record, refer to the next chapter.

SOCIAL SECURITY

While your Social Security Number may be utilized to execute other types of identity theft, Social Security identity

---

37   <http://www.dmv.org/driving-records.php>

theft is when someone steals your SSN and uses it to obtain employment in your name. The primary way to detect this type of theft is to review your Social Security Statement (Form SSA-7005), which is mailed yearly, for accuracy. You can also request this statement at any time by calling the Social Security Administration: 1.800.772.1213 or online at https://secure.ssa. gov/apps6z/isss/main.html. If there are any discrepancies with this statement, then refer to the next chapter.

CRIMINAL

This type of identity theft is the most difficult to detect. There are so many disparate criminal records systems and databases that it is difficult to detect even if you are diligent. There is no substitute to examining records at courthouses, but it is also impossible to complete a nationwide search with this method. So, if you have a concern of criminal identity theft within one jurisdiction, then work with this jurisdiction to obtain your records. However, if you seek a nationwide criminal records search, then the system I have found to have aggregated the most comprehensive set of records is online through Background Check By SSN from Intelius.[38] As of this writing, the cost of this product was $49.95. There are less expensive options, but they do not have as much information and there is a greater chance of obtaining the wrong records since your SSN is not utilized. If there are any discrepancies between this record and your actual records, then refer to the next chapter.

---

38   "Background Check By SSN." Intelius. <http://www.intelius. com/background-check-ssn.html?trackit=171>

Chapter 6

Identity Theft Defense Strategies and Tactics: Recovery

This is by far my least favorite component of the overall identity theft strategy because this is where the most pain is felt. Unfortunately, it is the component that receives the most focus because nearly all devote zero or an inadequate amount of attention to the most important component: *prevention.* It is not too difficult or painful to shred your credit card receipts or pay a company $10 per month to assist you in placing fraud alerts on your credit report, but it is *extremely* painful to receive constant phone calls from annoying collection companies for debts that do not belong to you. To make matters worse, it seems like nobody wants to help you, and it can take a long time to recover. It is like someone runs a car into your house and it is completely your responsibility to clean up the mess. You exhaust vast amounts of needless energy, capital, frustration, embarrassment and you are left asking, "Why me?"

The Identity Theft Resource Center describes the emotional impact:

> Without intervention, some victims can become so chronologically dysfunctional that they are unable to cope any longer. They may

be severely depressed—some symptoms are exhaustion, overeating, anxiety, forgetfulness, or an unwillingness to leave home or their bed.[39]

Even with the substantial *pain* consideration, the least amount of our attention should be focused on *recovery* for three reasons[40]:

1. It is better to avoid a bad situation than to have to fix it. Enough said.

2. This component of the overall identity theft strategy is reactive (whereas prevention is purely proactive and detection is moderately proactive). Anything that is proactive requires knowledge "prior to" in order to effectively execute. If you do not know what do, then you cannot do it. Contrarily, items that are reactive do not require knowledge "prior to." Intelligent strategies concentrate on avoiding bad events and then knowing what to do (or knowing where to find "what to do") just "in case" of an undesired circumstance. In other words, you can "learn as you go" with this component as long as you have a fundamental understanding of the structure of *recovery*.

3. There are infinite combinations and permutations

---

39   "Fact Sheet." Identity Theft Resource Center. <http://www. idtheftcenter.org/artman2/publish/v_fact_sheets/Fact_Sheet_108_ Overcoming_The_Emotional_Impact.shtml>

40   When I state "the least amount of attention should be focused on recovery," I mean this not in the sense of the least amount of pages or words in this book devoted to this subject; rather, I mean time and resource allocation towards *recovery* versus *prevention* (or even *detection*).

of recovery processes. Individual identity theft cases are so unique and fluid that it is impossible to determine the exact optimal process for each case. It is more important to know the general guidelines for each situation rather than try to prepare for each and every possibility.

There are two things that you should do to be prepared for recovery: 1) Photocopy everything in your wallet and important identification documents along with contact information and store in a safe, secure location (not the same location as you keep the original documents—do not keep the photocopy of your driver's license in your wallet if that is where you keep your driver's license). This includes (but is not limited to) your driver's license, credit and/or debit cards, passport, SS card and health insurance card. The time between identity theft and closing infected accounts is like the first 48 hours after a homicide. This time is precious and irreplaceable. 2) Backup your computer system. If your identity is stolen and your system either crashes or is hijacked, then the recovery process is easier because you likely have information that is critical to recovering your identity.

With the proper knowledge (which I will present) and a little discipline (you are on your own for this one), a vast majority of identity theft recovery steps can be completed by yourself and without legal assistance (when legal assistance is necessary, it is *extremely* important to have the proper representation). It is necessary to treat this process as a part-time job and always take copious notes. It stinks that you are in this position, but your primary goals are to minimize the damage and get out of the situation as quickly as possible. So, focusing any effort on "why did this happen to me?" provides no benefit and only makes matters worse.

There are many services and experts that indiscriminately group the recovery tactics together regardless of type of theft. However, your actions (and order of actions) are dictated by the type of theft, despite the fact that there are many common elements in every type of theft. We will consider the necessary recovery steps in the same order that we discussed the different types of identity theft:

1. Financial
2. Medical
3. Driver's License
4. Social Security
5. Criminal

FINANCIAL IDENTITY THEFT

You received a phone call from a collection agency for a debt that does not belong to you. You fear that you may be a victim of identity theft…so what do you do?

1. Place a fraud alert on your credit report. (If you are practicing good prevention tactics or are enrolled with IDCuffs.com, then this is already completed, and you may not even be in this situation.) The first step assists to make certain no new damage can happen while completing the other steps (or at least minimizes the likelihood). If you are injured in a battle, your primary concern is to get out of the

battle, and then deal with the injury once you have reached a point of safety.

Equifax: 877.576.5734; www.alerts.equifax.com
Experian: 888.397.3742; www.experian.com/fraud
TransUnion: 800.680.7289; www.transunion.com

2. Review your credit reports for unauthorized activity. Get a copy from all of the three credit bureaus for free at www.annualcreditreport.com. It is important to get all three because they do not share information. So, what reports with one bureau may not report on another and that's the reason why you have three different credit scores—each company evaluates different data. If you are having issues obtaining free reports online, then go to another site and pay for it. It is unfortunate you have to incur this expense, but at this point Pandora's box has been opened and you need to close it ASAP. Review *everything* in your credit report and take detailed notes of *anything* that is inaccurate. Be prepared to discover many errors because 79 percent of credit reports contain errors.[41]

Author's Note: I have literally reviewed tens of thousands of credit reports and have noticed a mistake on more than 99 percent of the reports. About the only reports I did not notice a mistake on (and this

---

41   "Mistakes Do Happen: A Look at Errors in Consumer Credit Reports." United States Public Interest Research Group, Executive Summary. June 17, 2004. <http://www.uspirg.org/home/reports/report-archives/financial-privacy--security/financial-privacy--security/mistakes-do-happen-a-look-at-errors-in-consumer-credit-reports>

was infrequent) were those of relatively new credit consumers with very limited information. I know the bureaus publish studies that greatly diminish the percentage with errors, but like their credit reports, 99 percent of these studies are erroneous.

3. Close accounts you know or believe to be fraudulent. This is the point where you start addressing the injury, and it is helpful if you brought with you a first aid kit. The first aid kit, for our purposes, is the photocopy of all of your accounts with contact information. For new fraudulent accounts, finding contact information is relatively easy by simply taking the company name listed on the credit report and entering it into a search engine. At this point, do not bother calling collection companies and trying to "close the account" because this requires a little more work (and you may poke a sleeping bear).

4. File an Identity Theft Report with local law enforcement.[42] This report is what will provide you the legal authority to remove fraudulent debts both with the creditors and the credit reporting agencies. Be prepared to provide detailed information about the fraudulent activity (account names, account numbers, etc.) as well as information about the

---

42   This is to be done if and only if you are legitimately a victim of identity theft. If you simply have a few bills you want to rid from your credit report, this is not the proper method as you have committed a felony and are subject to harsh criminal penalties, including jail.

perpetrator, if you know or have an idea (most identity theft is committed by a person known by the victim). Make certain to keep a copy of the report for your records.

5. Submit a copy of the Identity Theft Report along with a letter requesting fraudulent accounts to be blocked to each bureau. Providing each bureau this report, letter *and* proper identification *requires* the bureaus to *block* this information. This component (along with Step #6) involves the most time and detail. The system and the bureaus are inherently difficult to work with, and you need to precisely follow this process in order to achieve the desired results. You need one document that verifies your SSN (such as your SS card or W-2) and two documents that validate your *current* address (such as your driver's license and/or utility bill). Make photocopies, enlarge and lighten the documents. Remember, the bureaus are always seeking a reason to take no action and a common reason for "no action" is illegible identification documents or claiming the dispute is frivolous. Submit the Identity Theft Report, identification documents and a letter (with complete name, address and SSN—do not place in your mailbox to send out!) explaining you are a victim of identity theft and request the specific fraudulent accounts be blocked.

Equifax
P.O. Box 740250
Atlanta, GA 30374

Experian
P.O. Box 1017
Allen, TX 75013

TransUnion
P.O. Box 6790
Fullerton, CA 92634

*Author's Note: It is my opinion that Experian is by far the worst credit reporting agency when evaluating customer service; Equifax is by far the best and TransUnion is in the middle. This opinion is based on my personal experiences, which include: 1) Ease of contacting. If you want to get a live representative with Experian, it requires several key strokes and considerable time, whereas with the other bureaus, it is one stroke. 2) Ease of finding necessary information. Try finding the **right** address to submit this identity theft report with Experian—it is actually easier to find Experian's information on Equifax's site! 3) Service when contacting. Equifax has always been pleasant and does not treat the consumer as a criminal. 4) Miscellaneous. Experian often does not originally consider disputes because they claim the dispute is frivolous or the proper identification documents were not submitted even though the opposite is true. You cannot accept "no" for an answer from them, and if this is the situation you encounter, then continue to dispute with stronger language. Whenever possible, I take my business to Equifax and encourage others to do the same.*

6. Submit Identity Theft Report and removal letter to creditors. This is the step that actually has the fraudulent information removed (whereas Step #5 has the fraudulent information blocked). This letter is similar to the letter sent to the bureaus, but it should only include the fraudulent account(s) held by the creditor, and it needs to request removal of the account (instead of blocking). Many creditors have fraud divisions and the contact information is easily accessible via a search engine. Even though the creditors may not require identification documentation, it is a good idea to also include it with the correspondence.

While collection companies are included in this step, they often require a little more attention and persistence. Even though the agencies are required by law to delete the fraudulent account (without cost to you), they do not always behave in this manner. If you are having issues with collection companies hassling you over fraudulent debts, then send a cease and desist letter.[43] This requires the agency to stop calling you; however, it does *not* eliminate the debt. So, continue to work with them until you achieve proper resolution.

7. File an Identity Theft Complaint with the Federal Trade Commission and your State Attorney General's Office. This step does not actually assist with your recovery efforts; however, it assists with

---

43   I have included a sample cease and desist letter in the Appendix of this book.

"detecting patterns of wrongdoing, and lead(s) to investigations and prosecutions."[44] The complaint with the FTC is easy, quick and can be completed online at: https://www.ftccomplaintassistant.gov/FTC_Wizard. aspx?Lang=en

This website provides contact information for each State Attorney General: http://www.consumerfraudreporting.org/stateattorneygenerallist.php

As previously mentioned, there are many different *recovery* processes for each type of identity theft and subgroups, too. The aforementioned is the general process for financial identity theft; however, if you encounter other types of financial identity theft, including bankruptcy fraud or investment fraud, then the following website is a good resource: http://www.ftc.gov/bcp/edu/microsites/idtheft/consumers/resolving-specific-id-theft-problems.html

MEDICAL IDENTITY THEFT

You just applied for health insurance and were denied due to a condition you do not have. While financial identity theft is a nuisance and aggravating, you may be victim of another type of identity theft that can jeopardize your life. You must first go through the process listed for medical identity theft in the *detection* section. You can only start the *recovery* segment *after* you have identified the theft.

The first priority is to remove the fraudulent information from your medical records, and the second priority is to remove the information from your insurance records.

---

44   "Identity Theft Complaint." Federal Trade Commission. <https://www.ftccomplaintassistant.gov/>

Furthermore, a HIPAA-covered entity is not required to remove incorrect information; rather, they can amend the records to show the correct information and denote the incorrect information. The reason for this policy is legal and medical. If correct information is erroneously deleted from the records, then:

1. A doctor can be sued for the subsequent diagnosis and treatment as the reason for the diagnosis has been deleted.

2. If complications arise from the treatment, then the doctor needs to know the treatment in order to take proper counteractions.

Also, remember that the rules and rights for medical identity theft victims are not as strong or as clear as the rights for financial identity theft victims. The first step is to send a letter to the health provider requesting the amendment or removal of fraudulent information. The following is a sample letter from the World Privacy Forum (which is the recognized leader in regards to medical identity theft):

> *I may be a victim of medical identity theft. Some one may have obtained medical services using my name or my health insurance. The medical records that your institution maintains about me may include information that is actually about some one else. That information could be used to adversely affect my personal health care or to deny me insurance benefits that I am entitled to receive. I am working to identify the effects of the medical identity theft and to*

remove incorrect information from my files. Your institution not only has a responsibility to maintain accurate records, but it too may have been a victim of the same identity theft. We have a joint interest in resolving this problem. You may want to report my request to the part of your organization responsible for health care fraud.[45]

After this verbiage, it is appropriate to list the specific fraudulent information. If the provider makes the amendment, then it must also inform you of what it did as well as make reasonable efforts to inform others about the amendment in a reasonable amount of time. It is important to request an accounting of disclosures that informs you of the date of the disclosure, the name of the person or entity to whom it was disclosed, a brief description of the information disclosed and a brief statement of the purpose of the disclosure.

You must verify that the appropriate parties have been notified to make certain others are not relying on the original incorrect or fraudulent information. *Appropriate parties* include insurers, other medical providers and/or possibly employers. If an appropriate party was not included, then you need to request with the original provider to inform this party.

After you have confirmed that all the appropriate parties have been informed, *then* you must verify they took the

---

45   Robert Gellman. "Access, Amendment, and Accounting of Disclosures: FAQs for Medical ID Theft Victims." World Privacy Forum. March 18, 2008. <http://www.worldprivacyforum.org/FAQ_medicalrecordprivacy.html>

corrective actions to remove/amend the faulty information. This can be a matter of life and death, so it is prudent not to rely on their employees or internal systems.

If your issues are not resolved at this point, then there are other rights and remedies available; however, it makes sense to consider legal counsel. It is very important to provide counsel your detailed notes including all action you have taken, correspondence and names and date of the people with whom you spoke.

DRIVER'S LICENSE IDENTITY THEFT

You get a summons to appear in court for a DUI that you did not commit. Uh-oh, either there is a clerical error or you are the victim of driver's license identity theft. After you have completed the steps listed in the driver's license identity theft detection section, then you can start to *recover* your identity. Each state has different rules regarding the next steps, so you must research the process for your particular state either by contacting your Secretary of State or searching online. Generally it involves speaking with someone at your DMV (possibly scheduling an appointment), submitting a statement detailing the fraud and supporting documents (identity theft report, identity validation documents, etc.) and then achieving resolution.

The desired result is to have the fraudulent information deleted and make certain your driver's license number is secure going forward. Some states allow you to change your driver's license number (and this should be your preference if it has been compromised), and others do not. Minimally, you should contact your local DMV to request the "verify ID" option (this would have already been completed and you may not be in this situation if you had followed a *prevention* tactic). States that have this option require officers and licensing agents to request two forms of identity for validation.

SOCIAL SECURITY IDENTITY THEFT

You receive your yearly Social Security Statement and realize your listed income is *way* more than you earned. While it would have been nice to have that money, most likely someone has committed SS identity theft. Call the SSA (1.800.772.1213 between 7am–7pm, Mon–Fri) to review the earnings with a representative. If there is a discrepancy, then they will refer you to a Social Security field office to launch an investigation. Do not expect the SSA to provide too much assistance to resolve the issue. Social Security identity theft tends to help the victim as overstated earnings increases Social Security benefits (this is not considering tax implications, which the SSA properly considers the IRS's issue); so, the SSA tends to take a hands-off approach to SS identity theft restoration. This is reflective in many of their policies and information regarding identity theft.

The SSA website regarding identity theft is a perfect example: for "Actions to take in the case of identity theft"[46] it is first recommended (in the case of a stolen card which starts the section of "What can I do in the case of identity theft?") that you "apply for a replacement card." Replacing a Social Security card is far down on the list of priorities when your identity is in jeopardy. The next recommended step is to "review your earnings records (with SSA) to ensure they are correct and that no one else is using your

---

46   "Actions to Take in the Case of Identity Theft." Social Security Administration.   <http://ssa-custhelp.ssa.gov/app/answers/detail/a_ id/625/kw/identity%20theft%20investigation 07/12/2010>

number to work." So while you are gathering the proper documents and completing an application for a new Social Security Card, waiting for your number to be called at a branch office and then finally speaking with a SS representative to determine if someone is artificially increasing your earnings and benefits, the perpetrator is in Tahiti sipping on Pina Coladas and watching the dolphins.

Author's Note: The Social Security Administration does not have intelligent identity theft policies. There are other examples of misguided and laissez-faire policies of the SSA, but it is appropriate to cover them in the last chapter where I disclose many of my personal insights and experiences. Even though most experts, the FTC and the SSA recommend "working with your local Social Security office to resolve the issue," I could not make this recommendation without the caveat of what to expect when working with the SSA.

CRIMINAL IDENTITY THEFT

Your doors are busted down by a SWAT team in the middle of morning, you are thrown out of your bed and the next thing you know you are on the floor with your hands handcuffed behind your back. There is a warrant out for your arrest for drug trafficking. This may seem a little sensational, but it could happen. While you are probably not going to convince the arresting officers that you are a victim of identity theft, after you are released, it is a good idea to restore your name, which can be started after you have completed the steps listed in the criminal *detection* section.

The restoration process is a two-step process: 1) prove innocence and 2) clear name from databases and/or criminal justice computer systems. In addition to the obvious hurdles to these tasks, it is compounded due to the inconsistent procedures of each state (and even jurisdiction) and their disparate computer systems. For these reasons, it is absolutely critical that you keep a detailed log of all conversations with names, phone numbers, addresses and e-mail addresses. In addition to this log, make certain to keep all correspondence in a secure location and always send letters via certified mail with return receipt. The following is the general process:

1. Contact the arresting law enforcement agency, such as your local police department, if they are the arresting law enforcement agency. Explain the situation, and request to have your identity cleared and restored. If you are able to clear your name this easily, you are lucky and should go buy a lottery ticket. Most likely, you are just beginning the process.

2. Get as much detail about the crime and perpetrator as possible. Find out the "who, what, where and when" of the crime. Also find out what biometric data (fingerprints, mug shot, signature, height, weight, marks, etc.) and identification documentation were collected from the perpetrator.

3. File an Identity Theft Report with your local law enforcement agency. This may also be called a False Impersonator Report. Request that the agency collect biometric data (same as listed in #2) and identification (driver's license or passport) to confirm your identity *and* forward to the arresting law enforcement agency.

4. Request that the arresting law enforcement agency compare biometric and identification documentation (included in the Identity Theft Report) to that of the perpetrator and issue a Clearance Letter. Make certain this agency also recalls any warrants. The Clearance Letter (which is sometimes referred to as a Certificate of Release) is something you will need to keep on you at all times until you are certain your name has been fully restored. Due to the aforementioned disparate systems, you may have been "cleared," but not all databases accurately reflect this result. This letter informs future officers of your innocence.

5. Request that the arresting law enforcement agency restore your name with the appropriate parties and databases. The agency must: 1) forward the Clearance Letter to all city, county, state and federal databases, 2) change all records from your name to the perpetrator's name or John Doe if the perpetrator's name is unknown and 3) file for an investigation with the District Attorney (or court of jurisdiction).

6. Work with the court to clear your name from court records. A judge is required to make this determination, but you need to consult the laws of your state in order execute this step. The following is required from the court: 1) declaration that you are factually innocent, 2) an action to change the name on the arrest records and the warrants of the arrest to the perpetrator (or John Doe if unknown) and 3) written verification of innocence for you to carry.

If you are a victim of criminal identity theft, it is even more important for you to frequently review your criminal records for *detection*. If issues persist, then you must repeat the *recovery* steps. Restoring an identity from criminal identity theft is the most legal-intensive restoration process. Depending on the severity of the crime, the depth of the identity theft and the results you are able to personally achieve, you may want to consider legal representation.

Chapter 7

Miscellaneous Identity Theft Concepts

We have discussed in great detail the overall identity theft defense strategy including specific tactics for *prevention, detection* and *recovery*. If you learn and practice these tactics, then you are amongst the top 1 percent of the populace for identity theft awareness and preparedness.

In this chapter, I consider concepts that do not necessarily fit squarely in the previous sections and/or were purposely omitted. I take a little more liberty to express my opinions, ideas and execution strategies, but I do not stray too far off the reservation.

The first thing you need to understand and accept is that the American identity system has huge issues, and there are very few parties who are *truly* interested in protecting your identity. In fact, there are many parties whom you trust that actually have motivation to keep your identity at risk! With this awareness, you can proceed to the next step, which is to develop an effective comprehensive *personal* defense strategy and that includes a breakdown into specific actionable tactics. It is necessary to distinguish *personal* because if your next step is to fight or complain about the system (at the expense of developing a personal strategy), then the only one who stands to lose is you. Nobody cares about you. Also, if you attempt to develop one *overall tactic* (i.e., credit monitoring) without breaking down into specific actionable tactics, then the result is an ineffective and non-comprehensive defense strategy.

Of course this defense strategy must be *front-end loaded* with the highest percentage of resources dedicated to *prevention* and the least proportion towards *recovery.*

Aside from identity abstinence, the best method of protecting your identity is to make certain that only you are using your identity.

I know this is a profound thought: if only I use it, then it is hard to lose. With all of the electronic and print data flowing around and the inability to personally secure the data, it is impossible to guarantee that only you will use your identity. However, if you can prevent others from *effectively* using your identity, then you have substantially completed your goal. When someone attempts to use your identity, then your identity is already stolen, but if you are able to prevent him or her from attaining the desired result from the stolen identity, then you have achieved your goal. The best method to prevent others from fraudulently using your identity is to have fraud alerts on your credit report.

Fraud alerts are the foundation of all effective identity theft defense strategies.

Even without the rights afforded to you by the Fair Credit Reporting Act, I believe the right to make certain your identity is affirmed prior to allowing another entity to use or access your identity is fundamental and self-evident. Accepting seven of nine Social Security digits as identity affirmation is nowhere close to a minimally acceptable level of affirmation (I do not care what type of algorithm proves successful affirmation—obviously it is incredibly flawed).

If you have had your identity stolen and have followed

the proper *recovery* process, including filing an Identity Theft Report, then you are eligible for an extended fraud alert for seven years. Submit the report and extended fraud alert request to the bureaus. Without the Identity Theft Report, the bureaus will not place you on an extended fraud alert status. If you decide you no longer desire fraud alerts (I am not certain why you would ever reach such a conclusion), then you can always remove yourself from the fraud alert list (and the bureaus are happy to execute such requests). Also, the bureaus are required to remove your name from prescreened offers of credit for five years.

If protecting your identity via fraud alerts and removing your name from prescreened offers of credit is good enough *after* identity theft, then why is not good enough *prior to*? The credit reporting agencies are caught in a catch-22 on this one because it is difficult to make an argument that effective means of defense should only be extended after your identity has been stolen. I discuss this in greater detail later, but here is a preview: CRAs earn income by *selling* your information. So, if you remove your name from the sales lists, then you decrease their income potential. Also, the valuable clients of the bureaus are the companies requesting credit on a regular basis. So, anything that makes their clients' lives more difficult (i.e., fraud alerts) is something they will fight against.

Credit Freezes

Another prevention tactic not previously considered is a security and/or credit freeze. The reason I do not recommend this tactic is because I consider it inferior to fraud alerts, and it needlessly impedes on your ability to utilize credit. Remember, I do not despise credit, the way it functions in our system or the sharing of data. To the contrary, I believe credit has become part of the infrastructure of our society (similar to the United States Postal Service) and provides tremendous opportunity but also carries with it considerable risk. As such, the credit *system* needs to be afforded the same consideration and protection as other vital components of our infrastructure, such as our power grid. I become frustrated when others do not hold credit in the same regard (because you cannot *see* or *touch* it), and I despise the resulting negative effects, such as needless identity theft.

Here are some of the reasons I do not recommend a credit freeze versus a fraud alert:

1. It often requires money to both place *and* remove a credit freeze. Fees range from $5–$20 (with an approximate average of $10) to both place *and* remove the freeze for *each* CRA. The fees differ from state to state and tend to be free for identity theft victims. It is my opinion that *any* service provided to prevent identity theft by the CRAs should be free. If you want to pay another company to execute this free service as a convenience, then this is your prerogative. This also includes free credit monitoring if you desire it! You are paying them to do their job of keeping accurate data! The following provides a detailed list of fees by state for credit freezes: https://help.equifax.com/app/answers/detail/a_id/75/search/1

2. It requires extra steps that should not be your burden. When you have a credit freeze and want to apply for credit, then **you** are responsible for lift-

ing the freeze with each bureau and then reinstating with each bureau. When you are applying for credit, you are indicating you wish to become a client of the credit provider; thus, this "security layer" should be a company's task and expense, as is the case with fraud alerts (the creditor is responsible for contacting you to verify it is *really you* applying for credit).

3. Credit freezes require the consumer to initially set or permanently lift the freeze with *each* Credit Reporting Agency (CRA); whereas, fraud alerts only require contacting one CRA.

4. You may not be able to access credit when you want and/or need it. To apply and be granted credit, you must first lift the freeze with each bureau. For example, in certain circumstances, you may not be able to lift the freeze via the phone during non-business hours.

5. Turning something *on* and *off* presents more opportunity for human error and thus greater risk of identity theft. If you temporarily lifted the freezes, applied for credit and then forgot to reset the freezes with each bureau, then you are vulnerable. With fraud alerts, there is no *on* and *off*.

6. You may lose your chance of employment. If a potential employer requires access to your credit report, and you do not lift the freeze, then they may pass on you. Whereas, with a fraud alert, the potential employer is still allowed access to your credit.

7. It ensures no fraud prevention controls for existing accounts or relationships. A fraud alert requires reasonable verification steps for a new credit line, extension of credit or requesting a higher limit on the card when accessing credit. A credit freeze does not prevent or diminish the chances of any of those.

8. It doesn't secure issuing credit, just accessing credit reports. If someone else has your PIN and lifts the freezes, then the CRAs will go through the normal, unsecure procedures without confirming that *you are who you say you are.*

I do not think credit freezes are horrible, and they are certainly better than no layer of security prior to extending credit. For the aforementioned reasons, I consider credit freezes to be an inferior option to fraud alerts. It misdiagnoses the issue as it prevents access to credit information, but it does not stop the extension of fraudulent credit.

Insurance and Legal Representation

Two considerations not fully explored are legal representation and insurance. Let's start with the easier of the two: insurance. If the insurance product does not cover you regardless of fault and does not provide legal assistance with restoration, then I do not recommend it (and believe it is worthless). The first consideration that should raise suspicion is the fact that the insurance is offered by the very same companies that fail to protect your identity. Additionally, *the insurance does not cover monies stolen from you.* While there may be entities other than you who are financially responsible for the theft, it is not the insurance companies. Some policies pay expenses such as lost wages (with a limit normally capped at $2,000). In addition to all of the paperwork to restore your credit, it is necessary to complete more paperwork to claim insurance. It just does not seem worth it.

Legal representation that is included with insurance *may* be worth it. Beneficial legal representation included in an insurance plan is comparable to *catastrophic insurance.* Regardless of how it is marketed, most restoration efforts do not require legal or any type of assistance. It requires knowledge (most of what you need is contained in this book), patience, discipline and follow-through. Consumers mistakenly believe that if they have restoration insurance (legal or non-legal) that the representatives will restore their identity for them. This is not reality. Most likely, they will advise or read the processes similar to the ones contained in this book (and they are probably not as thorough as the ones I have provided). So, for most types of identity theft restoration, insurance is not necessary. Additionally, many homeowner's insurance policies and credit card companies also provide identity theft insurance as part of your policy or program.

The main reason for legal representation is criminal identity theft. If you think it is worthwhile to pay a monthly amount so that you have coverage for this type of identity theft, then I recommend a plan from Prepaid Legal Services, Inc., as they offer meaningful *legal representation.* This service costs $10–$15 per month, and it also includes credit monitoring (albeit it is only from Experian). By purchasing such a protection or service, you insure yourself against the legal bills associated with *catastrophic* identity theft, which can exceed $5,000. I still advise you to start with *prevention* tactics, but this sort of offering as a supplement to prevention nicely rounds out the overall strategy. If you were to buy one prevention product and one detection and/ or recovery product, then IDCuffs.com and PrePaid Legal present an optimum tandem of value.

Guarantees

You should run away quickly from any company that offers a "guarantee." Why? If it is not abundantly clear by this point that there is no way to guarantee that your identity will not be stolen, then either you are not paying attention or I have failed miserably in conveying a very important idea. The magnificent casinos in Las Vegas were not built by giving away money to gamblers. Similarly, companies that offer guarantees do not increase their ROI by giving out money to victims of identity theft. Many of the famous *$1 million guarantees* are offering a *service* guarantee. The guarantee does not mean that if your identity is stolen that you will receive $1 million. On the contrary, if there is failure for them to perform their tasks, which leads to the theft of your identity, then they will spend up to $1 million dollars to repair your identity. How do you prove a failure of the service led to the theft of your identity? You don't.

From personal experience, almost everybody I have consulted believes such guarantees mean that if your identity is stolen that you receive $1 million. At best, this is deceptive advertising. At worst, this is preying on the unknowing and vulnerable. Either way, if a company is not completely transparent about the product, service or guarantees, then one can only imagine the effectiveness of the service being performed *behind the curtain* that you have no way of monitoring or judging.

Database Monitoring

I do not consider these services worthwhile. First, it definitely falls under *detection* and not *prevention*. Second, similar to credit monitoring, there are many false negatives and the users become fatigued of the already low-value alerts. Lastly, these databases do not indicate identity theft; they indicate anomalies of information. I have yet to see a study or a whitepaper that concludes that database monitoring measurably reduces identity theft. Are there instances where database monitoring has identified theft? Of course, but are they statistically significant? Are there enough timely databases with meaningful data, with proper indicator programs for identifying theft, such that the overall service is useful? I have not witnessed any such services or read any studies that logically reach such a conclusion. If this changes in the future, I'll be the first to amend my statement.

Identity theft is asymmetric. It is not clear who are your friends and who are your enemies. It is clear your identity is fundamentally important, and there are forces at work that pose significant risks to its security. This is why I consider identity theft the *exponential, multi-dimensional challenge*. I do not have an *optimal solution*; however, I have an *optimal structure* to the solution. It begins with a *true* understanding of the crime (and its different forms) and an effective defense strategy. Both of these have been considered and explained in this book. The next step is good execution of the strategy, which includes continual self-education. If you were to stop reading to focus on learning and practicing these concepts, it may serve your best interests. I would not be offended. However, if you have become an *identity theft junkie* and are craving more information, then continue on.

The following sections go into great detail about the laws and your rights and a brief discussion of a community identity theft defense program. Finally, I take off my restraints to factually expose the deceptive players in the industry as well as discuss relatively simple, common-sense solutions.

Chapter 8

Identity Theft and the Law

In order to develop effective strategies and tactics, it is necessary to understand the laws and consumer rights governing identity theft. This is the foundation from which to reverse engineer best practices. This is also where the misinformation and lack of understanding begins. So much of the information out there is focused on the sensational end results, popular heresy, mind-numbing statistics and exploitative self-promotion, and so little is dedicated to the facts, which begins with the laws and regulations.

Of course there are sources that consider bits and pieces of the various laws or regurgitate statutes, but I did not discover one centralized resource that effectively discusses the laws *and* their implications. I decided to develop this one centralized resource and present it here in this book. Such a resource does not exist because there are countless laws and statutes surrounding identity theft. You will soon learn that identity theft and the law is an incongruent quilt and that it was not stitched together with any rhyme or reason. Consumers, law enforcement officials and criminals alike are all confused by the laws concerning identity theft. However, there is a wealth of knowledge here that, when properly applied, assists with preventing your identity from being stolen.

For the reasons stated above, it is nearly impossible to logically present the laws relating to identity theft. Ordinarily, it would make sense to chronologically explain the development of the law. There are laws that are not directly intended to address identity theft (in other words, identity theft is treated like a byproduct of the law), and there are other laws with minor caveats concerning identity theft, like those concerning check fraud, for example. Some laws do not originally include sections related to identity theft but then have been amended to include such provisions. Finally, some laws were not specifically designed for identity theft but have had a greater impact than those that were. The approach I have adopted is to combine a little bit of both methods. I do not go into great detail of the laws; rather, I provide highlights of each.

Understanding the nuances of the identity theft laws is a crucial component to an effective defense plan. Defending yourself without this knowledge is equivocal to fighting a shadow—you cannot fight what you cannot see. If you are serious about avoiding identity theft victimization, then you must have an intimate knowledge of the laws that establish the rules of the game.

The Identity Theft and Assumption Deterrence Act (aka Identity Theft Act) was signed into law October 1998. This act amended 18 U.S.C. § 1028 to make it a federal crime when anyone "knowingly transfers or uses, without lawful authority, a means of identification of another person with the intent to commit, or to aid or abet, any unlawful activity that constitutes a violation of Federal law, or that constitutes a felony under any applicable State or local law."[47] Violations of the act are investigated by federal agencies such as the U.S. Secret Service, FBI and U.S. Postal Inspection Service and are prosecuted by the Department of Justice.

The act had two primary purposes:

1. Make the unlawful transfer of identity information a federal criminal offense.

2. Focus on consumers as *victims,* thus empowering and directing the FTC to:

   a. Log receipt of complaints of victims.

   b. Provide victims with information material.

   c. Refer complaints to the appropriate entities, including CRAs and law enforcement agencies.[48]

Prior to the passage of this act, identity theft was not specifically regulated or investigated as a crime. Law enforcement relied upon a few federal statutes to protect the information necessary to commit identity theft and upon general anti-fraud provisions to punish and redress any injury (such as the False Identity and Crime Control Act of 1982). Only when identity theft rose dramatically in the

---

47   Identity Theft and Assumption Deterrence Act of 1998. Section 3 (a) (7). 18 U.S.C. § 1028. October 30, 1998. <http://itlaw.wikia.com/wiki/Identity_Theft_and_Assumption_Deterrence_Act_of_1998#cite_ref-1>

48   Betsy Broder, Assistant Director for the Division of Planning and Information of the Bureau of Consumer Protection, Federal Trade Commission. Prepared statement of the Federal Trade Commission on Identity Theft Before the Committee on Banking and Financial Services United States House of Representatives. September 1, 2000.

1990s did Congress decide to address the issue directly.[49] The following punishments are detailed in the act:

- 5 years imprisonment if the resulting offenses obtain anything of value totaling $0–$999.

- 15 years if the resulting offenses obtain anything of value totaling $1,000 or more during any one-year period.

- 20 years if utilized to facilitate a drug trafficking crime or in connection with a crime of violence.

- 30 years if facilitating an act of domestic violence or international violence.

It also establishes that "any person who attempts or conspires to commit...shall be subject to the same penalties."[50]

The FTC logs complaints and lists in the yearly addition of the Consumer Sentinel Network Data Book (which is free to download at http://www.ftc.gov/sentinel/reports. shtml). In the 2009 edition, identity theft had the highest percentage of all complaints with 21 percent of the total. This is over two times the number of complaints received regarding collection companies (which was the second highest percentage of complaints)![51]

The act does not set up an apparatus for the target of identity theft to sue the thief directly. He or she must

---

49   Identity Theft and Assumption Deterrence Act of 1998. Section 3 (f). 18 U.S.C. § 1028. October 30, 1998. <http://itlaw.wikia.com/wiki/Identity_Theft_and_Assumption_Deterrence_Act_of_1998#cite_ref-1>

50   Ibid.

51   Consumer Sentinel Network Data Book for January – December 2009. February 2010. p 3.

convince a law enforcement agency to investigate and the Department of Justice to prosecute. Since the victim is often only *indirectly harmed* with indirect economic losses like attorney's fees and costs associated with correcting credit reports, he or she ordinarily cannot sue. Most importantly, it is difficult for anybody to seek restitution from a faceless thief.

The Identity Theft Penalty Enhancement Act was signed into law July 2004. This act amends and augments the Identity Theft Act to define and establish penalties for "aggravated identity theft, which is defined as during and in relation to any felony violation in subsection (c), knowingly transfers, possesses, or uses, without lawful authority, a means of identifying another person...and continues to establish the penalty as in addition to the punishment provided for such felony, be sentenced to a term of imprisonment of 2 years."[52]

In other words, if you use someone else's identity in conjunction with a felony, then there is a *mandatory* additional sentence of two years. If the felony is terrorism, then the additional *mandatory* sentence is five years. The reason the sentence is mandatory **and in addition to** the felony sentence is to prevent judges from exercising leniency when combining the two sentences together (as is often the case). The spirit of legislation is that you receive a punishment that fits the crime for the felony and there is an additional punishment (two years) that fits the additional crime.

This act also "appropriated to the Department of

---

52   Identity Theft Penalty Enhancement Act. Section 2 (a) (1). 18 U.S.C. § 1028. July 15, 2004.

Justice, for the investigation and prosecution of identity theft and related credit card and other fraud cases constituting felony violations of law, $2,000,000 for fiscal year 2005 and $2,000,000 for each of the 4 succeeding fiscal years."[53]

Of course, the DOJ requires funds to prosecute these cases, however, to provide perspective of how miniscule these appropriated funds are towards identity theft, in 2009 this translated to $0.18 per identity theft or fraud victim and 0.04 percent of the total dollar amount of fraud.[54] This soundly displays the disparity of resource commitment by the government and the scale and negative impact of the crime.

The Fair Credit Reporting Act (FCRA) was signed into law October 1970. This act "sets forth legal standard governing the collection, use, and communication of credit and other information about consumers."[55]

The FCRA was the first federal law to regulate the use of personal information (both consumer credit reports and investigative consumer reports) by private businesses. This law was enacted to regulate the growing credit reporting agencies (CRAs) that had amassed large amounts of consumer data, which sometimes was used to deny services or opportunities. Individual regulation led to widespread abuse by the CRAs, including requirements of filling quotas of

53   Identity Theft Penalty Enhancement Act. Section 6. 18 U.S.C. § 1028. July 15, 2004.

54   This is based on a report estimates of 11.1 victims and $54 billion total annual fraud as reported in the *2010 Identity Fraud Survey Report: Identity Fraud Continues to Rise – New Accounts Fraud Drivers Increase; Consumer Costs at an All-Time Low.* Javelin Strategy & Research.

55   The Fair Credit Reporting Act. Federal Trade Commission. <http://www.ftc.gov/os/2000/12/fcrafrn.pdf>

negative information on consumers! This was primarily accomplished through false and incomplete reporting.

Prior to passage of the FCRA, these reports commonly included *lifestyle* information on subjects, such as sexual orientation, drinking habits and cleanliness. Much of the information was outdated and providing the file to law enforcement was unauthorized. From the inception of credit reporting agencies in the late 1800s until the passage of this act in 1970, there was gross abuse of the public trust, which led to a congressional inquiry and federal regulations of the CRAs. The FCRA was spearheaded by Representative Leonor Sullivan and Senator William Proxmire.

The Consumer Credit Reform Act of 1996 significantly strengthened the FCRA by defining timeframes for handling accuracy disputes, duties of parties taking adverse actions, information contained in reports, duties of furnishers of information to CRAs and allowing sharing of information among affiliates (i.e., prescreened offers of credit) as long as opt out provisions were provided and conspicuous. It also limited the preemption of stronger state laws.

The FCRA set minimum federal protections, which the states could exceed. The 1996 amendments strengthened and defined these minimum standards, but also preempted states from enacting stronger laws. The amendment had an expiration clause of January 1, 2004.

The Fair and Accurate Credit Transactions Act (FACTA) of 2003 was signed into law December 2003 (just prior to the expiration of the preemption statutes of states set forth in the Consumer Credit Reform Act). This act has the most recent amendments to the FCRA. It reaffirmed the expiring provisions for the CRAs as well as the following new preemptions: annual free credit reports, credit score disclosure by CRAs and mortgage lenders when score is utilized for granting credit, risk-based pricing notices, opt out rights (regarding preapproved offers of credit), truncation of credit or debit card numbers on receipts, placement of fraud or active duty military alerts, blocking of information resulting from identity theft, prohibiting sale or collection of debts resulting from identity theft and disposal of records containing the information of credit reports.

This act provides consumers considerable power to take control of their personally identifying information (PII) and thus minimizes the risk of identity theft. Many of the identity theft defense tactics are made possible by this act, such as fraud alerts and the option to opt out of preapproved offers of credit. However, this act also establishes that it is the consumer's responsibility to activate these tactics. So, the consumer must place a fraud alert and request to be opted out of preapproved offers; it is not an "opt in" structure whereby the consumer would have to request to have the fraud alerts removed or request to receive preapproved offers of credit.

The Red Flag Rules (enforcement) are a component of FACTA. This component of FACTA establishes the legal framework requiring the federal banking agencies, the National Credit Union Administration and Federal Trade Commission to develop guidelines for the possible instances of identity theft. Even though FACTA was passed in 2003 and the Red Flag Rules were completed and approved on October 31, 2007, the enforcement of the Red Flag Rules has been delayed five times due to pushbacks by the opposition.

The following is an excerpt from the Fair Credit Reporting Act § 615 (e):

> *(1) Guidelines. The Federal banking agencies, the National Credit Union Administration, and the Commission (FTC) shall jointly, with respect to the entities that are subject to their respective enforcement authority under section 621 –*
>
> > *(A) establish and maintain guidelines for use by each financial institution and each creditor regarding identity theft with respect to account holders at, or customers of, such entities, and update such guidelines as often as necessary;*
> >
> > *(B) prescribe regulations requiring each financial institution and each creditor to establish reasonable policies and procedures for implementing the guidelines established pursuant to subparagraph (A), to identify possible risks to account holders or customers or to the safety and soundness of the institution or customers; and*
> >
> > *(C) prescribe regulations applicable to card issuers to ensure that, if a card issuer receives notification of a change of address for an existing account, and within a short period of time (during at least the first 30 days after such notification is received) receives a request for an additional or replacement card*

*for the same account, the card issuer may
not issue the additional or replacement card,
unless the card issuer, in accordance with
reasonable policies and procedures –*

*(i)   notifies the cardholder of the request
at the former address of the cardholder
and providers to the cardholder a
means of promptly reporting incorrect
address changes;*

*(ii)   notifies the cardholder of the request
by such of other means of communication as the cardholder and the card
issuer previously agreed to; or*

*(iii)   uses other means of assessing the
validity of the change of address, in
accordance with reasonable policies
and procedures established by the
card issuer in accordance with the
regulations prescribed under sub-
paragraph (B).*

(2) Criteria

*(A) In general. In developing the guidelines re-
quired by paragraph (1)(A), the agencies
described in paragraph (1) shall identify patterns, practices, and specific forms of activity
that indicate the possible existence of identity
theft.*

*(B) Inactive accounts. In developing the guidelines
required by paragraph (1)(A) the agencies de-*

scribed in paragraph (1) shall consider including reasonable guidelines providing that when a transaction occurs with respect to a credit or deposit account that has been inactive more than 2 years, the creditor or financial institution shall follow reasonable policies and procedures that provide for notice to be given to a consumer in a manner reasonably designed to reduce the likelihood of identity theft with respect to such account.

(3) *Consistency with verification requirements. Guidelines established pursuant to paragraph (1) shall not be inconsistent with policies and procedures required under section 5318 (1) of title 31, United States Code.*

The following is a summary from the FTC website:

The final rules require each financial institution and creditor that holds any consumer account, or other account for which there is a reasonably foreseeable risk of identity theft, to develop and implement an Identity Theft Prevention Program (Program) for combating identity theft in connection with new and existing accounts. The Program must include reasonable policies and procedures for detecting, preventing, and mitigating identity theft and enable a financial institution or creditor to:

1. *Identify relevant patterns, practices, and specific forms of activity that are "red flags" signaling possible identity theft and incorporate those red flags*

into the Program;

2. *Detect red flags that have been incorporated into the Program;*

3. *Respond appropriately to any red flags that are detected to prevent and mitigate identity theft; and*

4. *Ensure the Program is updated periodically to reflect changes in risks from identity theft.*

The agencies also issued guidelines to assist financial institutions and creditors in developing and implementing a Program, including a supplement that provides examples of red flags.

The final rules also require credit and debit card issuers to develop policies and procedures to assess the validity of a request for a change of address that is followed closely by a request for an additional or replacement card. In addition, the final rules require users of consumer reports to develop reasonable policies and procedures to apply when they receive a notice of address discrepancy from a consumer-reporting agency.[56]

It is difficult to develop and enforce rules across so many industries and businesses that vary in scope and size. The rules allow for designing and implementing programs that are appropriate to the size and complexity of the financial institutions and creditors. Similar to the

---

56   Red Flag Rules. Federal Trade Commission. <http://ftc.gov/opa/2007/10/redflag.shtm>

way the Privacy Control Act of 1974 helped to secure sensitive PII in the control of the government (this is discussed later), the rules guide businesses and creditors in identifying and acting upon *flags* in order to prevent and mitigate identity theft. It has taken considerable time to develop these rules, and after enforcement becomes effective, it will take even more time for substantial adoption. However, this is another tool to help secure your PII and thus is a positive step in the fight against identity theft.

The Electronic Fund Transfer Act was signed into law November 1978. This act "establishes the basic rights, liabilities, and responsibilities of consumers who use electronic fund transfer services and of financial institutions that offer these services. The primary objective of the act and this part is the protection of individual consumer engaging in electronic fund transfers."[57]

Electronic Fund Transfers (EFTs) include:

> *[T]ransfer of funds that is initiated through an electronic terminal, telephone, computer, or magnetic tape for the purpose of ordering, instructing, or authorizing a financial institution to debit or credit a consumer's account. The term includes, but is not limited to –*
>
> *(i) Point-of-sale transfers;*
>
> *(ii) Automated teller machine transfers;*
>
> *(iii) Direct deposits or withdrawals of funds;*

---

57   Electronic Funds Transfer Act. Section 2 (a) (1). 15 U.S.C. § 1693 *et seq.* July 15, 2004.

(iv) Transfers initiated by telephone; and

(v) Transfers resulting from debit card transactions, whether or not initiated through an electronic terminal.[58]

The act protects consumers who desire to engage in EFT services. The following are not covered by the act: checks, wire transfers, security and commodities transfers, automatic transfers or credit card transactions. This act establishes that consumers must be provided disclosures at the time they contract an EFT by the financial institution detailing the liability of consumers for unauthorized EFTs or the consumers have no liability, the institution must provide a specific telephone number and address for reporting lost or stolen access devices and it lists the procedure for resolving errors.

The act establishes that consumers may be held liable for portions of the loss resulting from the unauthorized EFT (assuming the financial institution provided the appropriate disclosures). The maximum liability depends on *when* the consumer notifies the financial institution of the unauthorized transaction. The extent of the consumer liability *cannot* be increased for any of the following reasons: 1) consumer negligence (i.e., wrote pin number on ATM card), 2) an agreement between consumer and financial institution allowing greater liability or 3) consumer liability is higher under state law.

The following is an chart that illustrates the liabilities and timeframes detailed in the law:

---

58   Electronic Funds Transfer Act. Section 2 (a) (1). 15 U.S.C. § 1693 *et seq*. July 15, 2004.

Consumer Liability

Timing Consumer Notifies Bank	Maximum Liability
Within 2 business days of learning of loss or theft.	Lesser of $50, OR total amount of unauthorized transfers.
More than 2 business days after learning of loss or theft or theft up to 60 calendar days after transmittal of statement showing first unauthorized transfer made with access device.	Lesser of $500, OR the sum of: (a) $50 or the total amount of unauthorized transfers occurring in the first 2 business days, whichever is less, **AND** (b) The amount of unauthorized transfers occurring after 2 business days and before notice to the institution.
More than 60 days after transmittal of statement showing first unauthorized transfer made with access device.	Lesser of $500, OR the sum of: (a) $50 or the total amount of unauthorized transfers occurring in the first two business days, whichever is less, AND (b) The amount of unauthorized transfers occurring after 2 business days and before notice to the institution. **AND** Unlimited liability for any transfer occurring after the 60-day period.

The Truth In Lending Act (TILA – Regulation Z), which was launched by the Consumer Credit Protection Act, was signed into law May 29, 1968. It has since had many amendments, with the most recent effective July 1, 2010. "The purpose of TILA is to assure a meaningful disclosure of credit terms so that the consumer will be able to compare more readily the various credit terms available to him and avoid the uniformed credit, and protect the consumer against inaccurate and unfair credit billing and credit card practices."[59]

It is important to note that while transactions consummated with a debit card or credit card may seem the same to the consumer (present card, verify and leave with product/service), the laws and liabilities are extremely different. TILA (e.g., credit transaction) provides superior protection versus EFTA (e.g., debit card transaction) as it provides consumers the legal right to get assistance from their banks with respect to amounts disputed with the merchant. For example, if a credit card holder orders merchandise and it is not delivered, the credit card-issuing bank is required to treat the matter as a billing error and resolve it. On the contrary, the card-issuing bank is *not* required to become involved if it is a debit or ACH transaction. The Automated Clearing Houses are only third party processors and liability and/or responsibility is limited to the processing component of the transaction.

Prior to the passage of this act, consumers were faced with a puzzling assortment of credit terms and rates, which made it difficult (nearly impossible) to compare the *true* costs of loans. This act established a uniform system for disclosures including standardization of credit terminology

---

59   Consumer Credit Protection Act. Truth In Lending Act, Reg Z. Codified to 15 U.S.C. 1601 § 102. Last amended July 1, 2010.

and expression of rates. The following are additional rights afforded by this act:

- Protects consumers against inaccurate and unfair credit billing and credit card practices.

- Provides consumers with rescission rights.

- Provides rates caps for certain dwelling-secured variable rate loans.

- Imposes limits on home equity lines of credit and certain closed-end mortgage loans.

This act is comprehensive and covers many different facets of consumer credit; however, for the purposes of this book, the focus is open-ended, *personal* credit transactions (business credit transactions are not covered in this act) and the pertinent identity theft components.

The Fair Credit Billing Act (FCBA) is an amendment of TILA signed into law July 1986. While TILA in its original form provided good initial steps, the FCBA "protects consumer(s) against inaccurate and unfair credit billing and credit card practices."[60]

The maximum liability for unauthorized charges is $50 *if* the charge is reported within 60 days (there is no liability if the card is reported lost or stolen prior to any unauthorized charges). Many consumers are aware of this maximum, but they are unaware that if the unauthorized charge is not reported within 60 days that the liability is not capped. FCBA provides better protections than EFTA

---

60   Consumer Credit Protection Act. Truth In Lending Act, Reg Z. Codified to 15 U.S.C. 1601 § 302. Fair Credit Billing Act. October 28, 1974.

as it has lower liability limits and covers more than unauthorized charges, including protection for goods or services that were not accepted or were not delivered as agreed, failure to post payment and other credits, such as returns and failure to send bills to current address. Additionally, if a creditor goes into bankruptcy prior to the delivery of goods or services, then there is no recourse under EFTA, and the same limits of liability ($50 for failure to provide goods or services) under FCBA. In essence, the credit card-issuing bank becomes your representative, mediator and bares part of the risk for charges that are "inaccurate or unfair."

The consumer dispute must be in writing and provide an explanation (and any supporting documents) detailing the inaccurate or unfair charges within 60 days of receipt after the first bill containing the error was mailed. The creditor must acknowledge the dispute within 30 days from receipt and resolve the dispute within two billing cycles (maximum 90 days). During the dispute process, the consumer does not need to pay the *disputed charges* and the creditor may not take any legal or other action during the investigation.

Reg E (EFTA) or Reg Z (TILA)?

Since transactions seem indifferent to the average consumer (and there is even some crossover), it is important to note the differences and application of the acts. If the unauthorized use of a combined access device-credit card (a credit card which requires a device to read) solely involves an extension of credit and does not involve an EFT (e.g., a card is used to draw cash advances directly from a credit line), then only Reg Z applies. If the unauthorized use of a combination access device-credit card involves only an

EFT (debit card purchases or cash withdrawals from an ATM from a checking account), then only Reg E applies. If the combined access device-credit card is stolen and unauthorized transactions are made by using the card as both a debit and a credit card, then Reg E applies to the unauthorized transactions in which the card was used as a debit card, and Reg Z applies to the unauthorized transactions in which the card was used as a credit card. In other words, the same card can have different rules applied to unauthorized charges depending on how it is used!

While the maximum liabilities are detailed in EFTA and TILA, both VISA USA and MasterCard International have instituted "zero liability" policies that are equally applicable to debit and credit transactions made through their networks, regardless of when they are notified. These policies 1) only relate to unauthorized transactions and not transactions that are later disputed (e.g., failure to provide the product), 2) can be revoked at any time and 3) do not apply to debit card processing associations.

In sum, as it relates to identity theft protection, TILA-FCBA provides superior protection versus EFTA, and so a consumer has better protection utilizing credit cards instead of debit cards.

The Fair Debt Collection Practices Act is an amendment of the Consumer Credit Protection Act and was signed into law September 1977. The purpose of the act is to "eliminate abusive debt collection practices by debt collectors, to insure that those debt collectors who refrain from using abusive debt collection practices are not competitively disadvantaged, and to promote consistent state action to protect consumers against debt abuses."[61] There are many rights established in this act, and the following are highlights:

Debt collectors may not:

- Communicate with consumers at times or places known to be inconvenient to consumers.

- Communicate by postcard or use any language or symbol on any envelope indicating that the contents relate to the collection of a debt.

- Communicate with third parties unless consented by consumer or allowed by court order.

- Communicate with the consumer if the consumer notifies the collector in writing of his or her refusal to pay the debt and instructs to cease further communication (unless advising the consumer further collection efforts are being ceased or that the collector may invoke specific remedies).

- Harass or abuse. The debt collector cannot –

  o Use threat of violence or other criminal means.
  o Use obscene or profane language.
  o Publicize a list of consumers who allegedly refuse to pay debt.
  o Advertisement of sale of debt to coerce payment.
  o Cause a telephone to ring repeatedly with intent to annoy, abuse or harass any person at the called number.

---

61   Fair Debt Collection Practices Act. 15 U.S.C. § 1692-1692o, Pub. L. 95-109, 91 Stat. 874, September 20, 1977.

- Provide false or misleading representations, such as an implication that the collector has any affiliation with the state or federal governments, incorrect amount or legal status of the debt, a threat to take any legal action unless action is intended to be taken, a false misrepresentation that the collector is an attorney or any communication or threatening to communicate to any person the credit information which is known or which should be known to be false, including the failure to communicate that a disputed debt is disputed.

Debt collectors must validate debt when requested and cease collection efforts if the debt is disputed. The act also establishes civil liabilities for collectors who fail to comply with the act, and also establishes the FTC for administrative enforcement of compliance of the act.

This act is particularly important for victims of identity theft because often they are forced to deal with fraudulent debt collections and unscrupulous debt collectors. Few victims (or even general consumers) understand their rights as it pertains to debt collections. It is a good idea to review this act and keep a copy handy if ever you are in the unfortunate situation of dealing with collectors.

The Electronic Signatures in Global and National Commerce Act (E-Sign Act) amends TILA and was signed into law June 2000. The act clarified that "a signature, contract, or other record relating to such transaction may not be denied legal effect, validity or enforcement solely because it is in electronic form."[62] In other words, the act clarifies that an electronic signature has the same legal meaning as a paper documents and a handwritten signature. The act also preserves the rights of individuals not to utilize electronic signatures by requiring a disclosure that the signatory has consented to the electronic format. Finally, if a law requires a business to retain signatures, the act establishes a requirement that is satisfied by retaining an electronic record, as long as the record *accurately reflects* the substance of the contract and can be accessed in an acceptable format for later reference.

The act provides great efficiencies, but it also raises new identity theft concerns since traditional methods of identifying a party and entering a legally binding transaction are normally absent. Typically, there is not a preexisting relationship and the parties are not engaging in the agreement face-to-face.

Uniform Commercial Code (U.C.C.) was first published in 1952 and **Article 4 – Bank Deposits and Collections, Section 406 – Relationship Between Payor Bank and its Customers and Section 103 – Variation by Agreement; Measure of Damages; Actions Constituting Ordinary Care,** which addresses identity theft in check fraud, was most recently revised in 1993. The U.C.C. is intended to provide some standardized guidance to states regarding laws dealing with sales and commercial transactions. Its goal is to provide substantial uniformity in commercial laws.

Section 406 considers the banks' reporting

---

62   Consumer Credit Protection Act. Truth In Lending Act, Reg Z. Codified to 15 U.S.C. 7001 § 101. Electronic Records and Signatures in Commerce Act. June 30, 2000.

responsibilities (statements) to its customers, the responsibilities and time requirements of customers in reporting unauthorized or fraudulent activity and the distribution of losses (depending on the actions of the customers and banks). The following are applicable excerpts from Section 406 as well as summaries:

> *(a) A bank that sends or makes available to a customer a statement of account showing payment of items for the account shall either return or make available to the customer the items paid or provide information in the statement of account sufficient to allow the customer reasonably to identify the items paid. The statement of account provides sufficient information if the item is described by item number, amount, and date of payment.*

Summary: Banks must provide access to statements and the ability to identify specific transactions.

> *(b) Purposefully omitted.*

> *(c) If a bank sends or makes available a statement of account or items pursuant to subsection (a), then customer must exercise reasonable promptness in examining the statement or the items to determine whether any payment was not authorized because of an alteration of an item or because a purported signature or items provided, the customer should reasonably have discovered unauthorized payment, the customer must promptly notify the bank of the relevant facts.*

Summary: Prompt Reconciliation: Customers must review statements and alert banks of unauthorized transactions in a reasonable time.

> *(d)* *If the bank proves that the customer failed, with respect to an item, to comply with the duties imposed on the customer by subsection (c), the customer is precluded from asserting against the bank:*
>
> > *(1)* *The customer's unauthorized signature or any alteration on the item, if the bank also proves that it suffered by a loss by reason of failure; and*
> >
> > *(2)* *The customer's unauthorized signature or alteration by the same wrongdoer on any other item paid in good faith by the bank if the payment was made before the bank received notice from the customer of the unauthorized signature or alteration and after the customer had been afforded a reasonable period of time, not exceeding 30 days, in which to examine the item or statement of account and notify the bank.*

Summary: This establishes the reasonable time at a *maximum* of 30 days from statement date in which to report the fraud before rights are forfeited. However, the timeline is extended in cases where banks do not exercise ordinary care (subsection e) or it can be shortened based on a contract (4-403). This also establishes the Repeater Rule whereby the customer is responsible if the same forger writes additional checks that are paid more than 30 days after the first statement date.

(e) If subsection (d) applies and the customer proves that the bank failed to exercise ordinary care in paying the item and that the failure substantially contributed to the loss, the loss is allocated between the customer precluded and the bank asserting the preclusion according to the extent to which the failure of the customer to comply with subsection (c) and the failure of the bank to exercise ordinary care contributed to the loss. If the customer proves that the bank did not pay the item in good faith, the preclusion on subsection (d) does not apply.

Summary: If fraud is not caught in reasonable time, but the bank failed to exercise ordinary care, which means *observance of reasonable commercial standards, prevailing in the area in which the person is located, with respect to the business in which the person is engaged,* then the loss is shared proportionally based on culpability between the bank and customer.

(f) Without regard to care or lack of care of either the customer or the bank, a customer who does not within one year after the statement or items are made available to the customer (subsection (a)) discover and report the customer's unauthorized signature on or any alteration on the items is precluded from asserting against the bank the unauthorized signature or alteration. If there is a preclusion under this subsection, the payor bank may not recover for breach of warranty under Section 4-208 with respect to the unauthorized signature or alteration to which the preclusion applies.

Summary: Regardless if the bank did not provide *reasonable care*, the customer has no claim against the bank after one year from the statement date.

This section clearly establishes that the prevention, detection and recovery from fraud/identity theft involving bank accounts is the responsibility of two parties and the resulting losses are proportionately distributed. If either party does not have *skin in the game*, then the motivation to *prevent, detect and recover* is substantially diminished. If the customer understands losses resulting from fraud are entirely the responsibility of the bank, then he or she is not going to exercise the same care as he or she does in a system where the risks are assigned according to proportional responsibility (and vice versa). While neither party desires fraud, this system provides motivation and incentive for each party to take proactive steps in preventing, detecting and recovering from fraud.

Section 103 provides for variances to Section 406 if the parties agree to such variances. This differs from TILA, which establishes rules (such as maximum liability for customer is $50 if the charge is reported within 60 days) and explicitly states no variances are allowed even if the parties agree to the variances (this is to prevent credit card companies from raising maximum customer liability in the fine print of the agreements).

> *(a) The effect of the provisions of this Article may be varied by agreement, by the parties to the agreement cannot disclaim a bank's responsibility for its lack of good faith or failure to exercise ordinary care or limit the measure of damages for the lack*

or the failure. However, the parties may determine by agreement the standards by which the bank's responsibility is to be measured if those standards are not manifestly unreasonable.

In other words, the bank's account agreements, aka fine print, can define and shorten *reasonable time* for statement review. Section 406 establishes reasonable time as "not exceeding 30 days"; however, it did not establish a *minimum* amount of time. This section allows an agreement to establish the amount of time afforded to customers to report unauthorized activity (it carves out cases of negligence and/ or when the bank does not exercise reasonable care).

This section was upheld in *Borowski v. FirStar Bank, Milwaukee, N.A.* in 1999.[63] Borowski had approximately $50,000 taken from his personal account by Liza Kazmarek, the woman whom he thought he was going to marry, through "forged checks, telephone transfers and handwritten notes." The account agreement stated:

You will promptly inspect Account statements. If you do not notify us of an unauthorized or altered item shown on your statement within fourteen (14) days of the statement date, you will lose any claim against us with regard to that item and any later items signed or altered by that same unauthorized party.

---

63   Jerrold A. Borowski and Jerrold A. Borowski, Personal Representative of the Estate of Anthony P. Borowski, *Plaintiffs-Appellants v. Firstar Bank Milwaukee, N.A.*, Defendant-Respondent, American Family Insurance Company and Allstate Insurance Company, Defendants. No. 96-3277 State of Wisconsin In Court Of Appeals, District I. February 10, 1998. Published Opinion Wisconsin Bar.

Borowski argued that Ms. Kazmarek was intercepting the statements and therefore was unaware of the unauthorized use of the account. The court concluded the 14-day timeframe for review to be reasonable and it was not the bank's responsibility to ensure *receipt* of the statements. The lesson from this case is that you should promptly review your statements within 7 days (not the 30 days discussed in Section 406), and if you do not receive the statements, then it is your responsibility to contact the bank in order to obtain a replacement copy.

Check Clearing for the 21ˢᵗ Century (Check 21 Act) was signed into law October 2003. The purpose of the act was to "facilitate check truncation by authorizing substitute checks, to foster innovation in the check collection system without mandating receipt of checks in electronic form, and to improve the overall efficiency of the Nation's payments system, and for other purposes."[64] Traditionally, banks physically moved paper checks from the bank where the checks were deposited to the bank that pays them. This process is inefficient and costly, and this act provides the legal structure for banks to handle checks electronically (which also means faster and more efficiently).

Highlights of Check 21:

- An electronic check with reproduction of both sides is an acceptable substitute for traditional, physical cancelled checks.
- The importance of having funds deposited and

---

64   Check Clearing for the 21ˢᵗ Century Act. 15 U.S.C. 5001. October 28, 2003.

available at the time of writing the check increased in importance as the typical timeline (which involved airplanes and trucks delivering the physical check to the paying bank) has been dramatically decreased. Checks are processed much more quickly when processed electronically.

• The customer is still provided the same legal protections with the substitute check as the original cancelled check.

The act certainly improves efficiency and reduces costs, but has some effects on fraud and identity theft. First, traditional check readers were designed to scan imprinted account and routing numbers rather than the physical, security features of the checks. Thieves were able to alter legitimate checks and in many scanners were unable to detect the forgeries. This loophole has been tightened (not closed) with the higher resolution of *real* scanners. Many retailers were able to transition to electronic check processing whereby the check is fed through a reader and processed like an account debit. An *approved* transaction created a false sense of security, and many clerks did not or do not request identity validation as was traditionally requested when submitting checks. Skipping this step increases the likelihood of identity theft and fraud.

Finally, electronic imaging has created considerable amounts of invaluable data information of which the online thieves target. Most have concluded that the electronic data actually decreases the risk of theft versus incredible amounts of unsecure physical checks being flown throughout the country (this is similar to the argument conclusion that it is safer to fly than drive—you may seem to have more control driving your own car, but statistics prove the fatality percentages are significantly higher when driving). The primary reason identity theft overall is reduced in the electronic world versus physical is because the "number of sets of eyes" reviewing the checks is decreased from approximately 30 to 5.[65]

This act is still relatively new and the impact is not fully understood; however, it is readily apparent that the use of credit cards instead of checks (physical or electronic) or debit cards provides consumers substantially more rights, protection and lower financial liability.

The False Claims Act (ch 67, 12 Stat. 696, aka Lincoln Law) was signed into law March 1863. This act establishes liability whenever someone (or an entity) fraudulently receives from or avoids payment to the federal government. The original purpose of the act was to hold unscrupulous defense contractors liable for providing bad mules to the government during the Civil War. The contractors fraudulently claimed the mules to be in good health, but upon delivery of the goods or mules, it was determined that the contractors had made fraudulent claims about the condition of the mules. This act assisted to control the rampant fraudulent contracts presented to the federal government during the Civil War. This was the first law that set the legal foundation for prosecuting identity theft.

---

65   "Check Clearing for the 21st Century Act." CSRSI. <http://www.csrsi.com/library/plugging-check-21-check-clearing-twenty-first-century-act>

The False Statements Act (18 U.S.C. 1001) was established June 1948. This was a culmination of the False Claims Act being collected, revised and divided many times. The act states:

> *Statements or entries generally*
>
> (a) *Except as otherwise provided in this section, whoever, in any matter within the jurisdiction of the executive, legislative, or judicial branch of Government of the United States, knowingly and willfully-*
>
> > (1) *Falsifies, conceals, or covers up by any trick, scheme, or device a material fact;*
> >
> > (2) *Makes any materially false, fictitious, or fraudulent statement or representation; or*
> >
> > (3) *Makes or uses any false writing or document knowing the same to contain any materially false, fictitious, or fraudulent statement or entry;*
>
> *shall be fined under this title, imprisoned not more than 5 years or, if the offense involves international or domestic terrorism (as defined in section 2331), imprisoned not more than 8 years, or both. If the matter relates to an offense under chapter 109A, 109B, 110, or 177, or section 1591, then the term of imprisonment imposed under this section shall be not more than 8 years.*[66]

The act made it a federal crime to lie to or conceal from a federal official.

---

[66]   False Statements Act. <http://www.law.cornell.edu/uscode/18/usc_sec_18_00001001----000-.html>

The False Identification Crime Control Act (18 U.S.C. § 1028 and 18 U.S.C. § 1738) was signed into law December 1982. (Section 1738 dealt with mailing private identification documents without a disclaimer; however, it has since been repealed by PL 106-578. Therefore, we do not consider this component of the act.) Chapter 1028 is titled "Fraud and related activity in connection with identification documents, authentication features, and information." This section is too lengthy for the purposes of this book; an overview is more appropriate.

Section 1028 prohibits any person from producing, transferring, or possessing any false *governmental* identification document or any document-making implement used for the production of false *governmental* identification. It does not include private identification documents, but it is a broad definition of *governmental documents*, including federal, state, local, foreign, international and quasi-international entities. It also establishes penalties for violations, such as a fine or imprisonment up to 30 years, or both.

The act was a culmination of a 10-year legislative process aimed at improving federal criminal statutes relating to the false identification problem and/or identity theft. It was based on a comprehensive study by the Department of Justice relating to the criminal use of false identification.

The Internet False Identification Prevention Act was signed into law December 2000. The act amends the False Identification Crime Control Act by prohibiting the transfer of a false identification document by electronic means, including on a template or computer file or disc. The main goal of the act was to end the distribution of counterfeit identification documents over the web. According to the FDIC, the act closed "a loophole by the ID Theft Act, enabling law enforcement agencies to pursue those who formerly could sell counterfeit social security cards legally by maintaining the fiction that such cards were 'novelties' rather than counterfeit documents."[67] In other words, the illegality and resulting punishment is the same if you e-mail a fraudulent Social Security card or if you provide a physical copy of a fraudulent Social Security card.

The Privacy Act (Public Law 95-579) was signed into law December 1974. The goal of the act is to secure the right of privacy with respect to confidential personal information held by the federal government. The act establishes:

- A basis for the correction of outdated or incorrect information.

- A limited extent to which records can be disclosed, which includes either authorization in writing from the citizen, court order or certain exceptions.

- Reasonable security safeguards that must be implemented by agencies for the handling of such data.

- That government agencies can only collect information that is relevant and necessary to accomplish the particular agency functions.

- That if a SSN is required, then the agency must inform you of what will be done with it and what the consequences are if you refuse to provide it.

In many ways, this act was forward thinking. As

---

67   "Putting an End to Account-Hijacking Identity Theft." Federal Deposit Insurance Corporation. <http://www.fdic.gov/consumers/consumer/idtheftstudy/legislative.html#fn51>

technology advanced in the 1960s and 1970s, there were escalating concerns about how databases might compromise individuals' privacy rights, which directly correlates to the proliferation of identity theft. The government realized that the less PII gathered, stored and disclosed translated into fewer cases of private information being compromised and thus fewer incidents of identity theft. While this act was a very positive step, it has its limitations as it does not address how PII is collected, distributed or stored by private industries, including data brokers, collection agencies, credit reporting agencies, etc. Have you ever noticed how infrequently government personnel records are compromised (relative to total number of records) versus private industry records? It is because the government has had 30 plus years of experience. It is only recently and with the advent of new regulations (e.g., the aforementioned Red Flag Rules) that the private industry is beginning to catch up and secure PII.

The Driver's Privacy Protection Act was signed into law in September 1994. The act establishes that a "State department of motor vehicles, and any officer, employee, or contractor thereof, shall not knowingly disclose or otherwise make available to any person or entity personal information about any individual obtained by the department in connection with motor vehicles record."[68] Prior to the passage of the act, it was possible to obtain a driver's full name, address, date of birth and driver's license number. This law was originally passed due to the stalking murder of the actress Rebecca Schaeffer. Her address was obtained by an obsessed fan by

---

68   Driver's Privacy Protection Act. 18 U.S.C. § 2721. September 13, 1994.

going through the records of the California Department of Motor Vehicles. Similar to many laws dealing with identity theft, this law was not passed specifically to combat identity theft; however, its positive implications on preventing identity theft are obvious.

The Shelby Amendment was signed into law June 2000. Shelby amended the Driver's Privacy Protection Act to include a provision that requires states to obtain a driver's express consent before releasing any personal information. While the Driver's Privacy Protection Act prevented acquiring a particular individual's PII, it allowed for acquiring/purchasing information in bulk from the DMV as long as there was an opt out feature. Senator Richard Shelby attached a provision to the transportation appropriations bill in 1999 that changed the opt out feature to an opt in feature. In other words, a consumer would have to request to allow his or her information to be sold in bulk.

The amendment met stiff opposition from many major lobbying organizations, including the Direct Marketing Association, state motor vehicle administrators, insurance companies and major car manufacturers (to name a few). Since opting in is so uncommon, this essentially stopped the practice of DMVs selling personal information. Despite the strong opposition, the Amendment was able to pass in large part because of the overall importance of the transportation bill. Imagine the outcry if the same type of feature were introduced requiring CRAs (or any organization that sells consumer data) to require consumers to opt in instead of the current opt out structure!

The Health Insurance Portability and Accountability Act was signed into law August 1996. The act was to "amend the Internal Revenue Code of 1986 to improve portability and continuity of health insurance coverage in the group and individual markets, to combat waste, fraud, and abuse in health insurance and health care delivery, to promote the use of medical savings accounts, to improve access to long-term care services and coverage, to simplify the administration of health insurance, and for other purposes."[69] The act is lengthy and comprehensive, but the two components most directly related to identity theft are the Privacy Rule (August 2002) and the Security Rule (April 2005).

The Privacy Rule provides protection of identifiable health information. It addresses confidentiality as well as specific technical safeguards of which companies covered under the act must implement a minimum of 20 standards to be compliant. It is similar to the Red Flag Rules in that it provides guidance to covered companies as to the areas that pose the greatest threat to identity theft, and the rule leaves it to the companies to determine a specific framework to combat (within the framework of the rule).

The confidentiality and safeguards required by companies to minimize incidents of identity theft are addressed in the Privacy Rule, and the Security Rule establishes the consumers' right to a copy of the account of disclosure records by health care providers and insurers. As discussed in the detection section, it is important to review these disclosures to verify the information is correct and not disclosed to any unwanted parties.

---

69   Health Insurance Portability and Accountability Act. Public Law 104-91. August 21, 1996.

While there is still a long way to go to ensure sound industry practices supporting *prevention, detection and recovery efforts*, the combination of these two rules is much better than the void that previously existed.

The Gramm-Leach-Bliley Act (aka the Financial Services Modernization Act) was signed into law in November 1999. The act was to "enhance competition in the financial services industry by providing a prudential framework for affiliation of banks, securities firms, insurance companies, and other financial service providers, and for other purposes."[70] The primary purpose of the act was to end regulations that prevented the merger of banks, securities firms, credit card companies and other financial services firms. This presented substantial risks, since the resulting financial institutions would have an enormous amount of PII without any regulation of its use!

There are three primary components of the act as it relates to identity theft: 1) Financial Privacy Rule, 2) Safeguards Rule and 3) Fraudulent Access to Financial Information Rule.

Financial Privacy Rule. This is the agreement between the consumer and the financial institution pertaining to the protection of the consumer's personal information. Institutions must provide the consumer with a privacy notice at the time the relationship is established, annually thereafter and whenever the policy is changed. The notice must explain what information is collected about the consumer, where the information is shared, how the information is used, how it is protected and also provide the option/instructions

---

70   Gramm-Leach-Bliley Act. Public Law 106-102. November 12, 1999.

for the consumer to opt out of information being shared with unaffiliated parties. The unaffiliated parties receiving consumer information are also subject to this rule. The Financial Services Regulatory Relief Act of 2006 amended the GLB Act to require agencies to propose a "succinct and comprehensible form" that allows consumers to easily compare the privacy practices of different financial institutions. In November 2009, eight federal regulatory agencies released the final model privacy notice.

Safeguards Rule. This rule is similar to the Red Flag Rules in that each financial institution is required to develop a written information security plan detailing how the company ensures the security and confidentiality of consumer information. The plan must:

1. Identify at least one employee to manage the plan and/or safeguards.

2. Perform a thorough risk management assessment of each department handling nonpublic information.

3. Develop, monitor and test the program to make certain it is effective.

4. Based on results and changes in technology and the industry, amend and/or continuously improve safeguards.

Fraudulent Access to Financial Institution Rule. The rule provides protection against "pretexting," which is the act of gaining personal nonpublic information under false pretenses. Often, thieves will act as though they are representatives of a financial institution (false pretenses) in order to gain personal information about the subject. This information is then used to steal the identity of the victim. This rule makes such an act illegal.

There are limitations to the act, since it is structured for the consumer to have an opt out instead of an opt in policy. Most consumers do not understand the complex laws and regulations and do not make informed decisions in regards to how their information is handled. These opt out policies are often difficult to understand, as the primary motive of the companies is to maximize profits, which means affording the minimum privacy rights and safeguards acceptable under the law (and sometimes less than what is dictated by law if they believe they can get away with it). Similar to many of laws, it is not perfect, but it is much better than the alternative of no privacy rights or safeguard policies.

The Identity Theft Enforcement and Restitution Act was signed into law January 2008. The act amends the Computer Fraud and Abuse Act of 1986 by authorizing restitution to victims at an "amount equal to the value of the time reasonably spent by the victim in an attempt to remediate the intended or actual harm incurred by the victim from the offense."[71] Even though restitution is authorized under this act, it is seldom collected as thieves are rarely captured (or have the restitution funds if captured). The act also provideds the federal government the authority to prosecute even if the criminal and victim are both located in the same state.

The Social Security Number Confidentiality Act was signed into law November 2000. The act "prohibit(s) the appearance of Social Security account numbers on or through un-

---

71   Identity Theft Enforcement and Restitution Act. 18 U.S.C. 1030 § 3663. January 3, 2008.

opened mailings of checks or other drafts issued on public money in the Treasury."[72] Prior to the issuance of the act, it was a common practice of the Treasury to provide SSNs on checks or visible on or through unopened mailings of government checks or drafts (such as tax returns). The SSN with name and address (and sometimes date of birth) is a gold mine for identity thieves, and the act prohibits this dangerous practice.

The Improved Security for Drivers' Licenses and Personal Identification Cards Act (aka the Real ID Act) was signed into law May 2005. The act requires driver's licenses and personal identification cards issued by the states to meet minimum standards outlined in the act in order for federal agencies to accept these documents for identity validation. The minimum standards are as follows:

> *(a) Minimum Document Requirements. – To meet the requirements of this section, a State shall include, at a minimum, the following information and features on each driver's license and identification card issued to a person by the State:*
>
> *(1) The person's full legal name.*
>
> *(2) The person's date of birth.*
>
> *(3) The person's gender.*
>
> *(4) The person's driver's license or identification number.*
>
> *(5) A digital photograph of the person.*
>
> *(6) The person's address of principle residence.*

---

72   Social Security Confidentiality Act of 2000. Public Law 106-433. November 6, 2000.

(7) The person's signature.

(8) Physical security features designed to prevent tampering, counterfeiting, or duplication of the document for fraudulent purposes.

(9) A common machine-readable technology, with defined minimum data elements.[73]

The act also details what is required to be presented *and* verified prior to issuance of the identification. There are additional security and safeguard requirements, including (but not limited to): 1) evidence person is legally in the U.S., 2) confirm with SSA that the SSN is the actual SSN of the individual, 3) establish fraudulent document training programs, 4) have a mandatory facial image capture, 5) make certain all persons producing the identification documents have the appropriate security clearance and 6) makes it a federal crime either to actually, or with intent, transport or transfer identification authentication features that are used on a document of the type intended or commonly presented for identification purposes.

The act requires states to meet these standards in order for their citizens to use their state-issued identification documents for federal purposes, such as boarding commercially operated airline flights, entering federal buildings and/or nuclear power plants. The act does not require states to change or adhere to these policies (this could be an infringement on state's rights); however, failure to comply does not allow their citizens to use the identification documents for federal purposes. In essence, states that do not comply render the identification documents useless except

---

73   Improved Security for Driver's Licenses and Personal Identification Cards Act. The Real ID Act. Public Law 109-13. May 11, 2005.

for state purposes and the specific purpose of the ID (such as identification for operating a motor vehicle).

The act was passed in response to the terrorist events of 9/11 as many of the terrorist had fake IDs, which would have been much more difficult to obtain or replicate had the act been in place. Prior to 9/11, neither major political party had an appetite for national standards for identification documents, and there was legislation with bipartisan support (that was thought likely to pass) that actually discouraged such standards. The mood drastically changed post-9/11 and the final report of the National Commission on Terrorist Attacks Upon the United States (9/11 Commission) recommended that "the Federal government should set standards for the issuance of birth certificates, and sources of identification, such as driver's licenses."[74]

There are concerns regarding the constitutionality of the act; specifically there are many who believe the act jeopardizes civil liberties. I provide my assessment of the overall impact of the act in the Chapter 9, but for now, let's consider the impact of the act on identity theft.

A nationally linked database allows millions of employees to access incredible amounts of personal information and documentation (not to mention the access to professional hackers) as the act requires storage of scanned copies of Social Security cards and birth certificates.

The authentication and verification of the documents utilized to obtain identification will make it more difficult for thieves to falsify documents and utilize said documents to obtain fraudulent identification from the DMV. Additionally, the tamper-resistant and secure cards will be

---

74   The 9/11 Commission Report: Final Report of the National Commission on Terrorist Attacks on the United States. 2004. p 390.

more difficult to counterfeit. Lastly, the state databases with photo images makes it more difficult to obtain fake IDs.

The act certainly makes it more difficult for thieves to acquire fraudulent IDs from DMVs as well as reproduce effective counterfeits, but it also vastly increases the amount of personal information and documentation stored and accessible via a computer.

Identity Theft and the Law: Conclusion

There are seamlessly endless laws, regulations and statutes that affect identity theft. It is not important to memorize every word of every law, but it is important to understand the basic premise of each law and know where to find more information if ever you encounter a situation requiring a deeper understanding. These laws empower you to take significant control of your identity by providing powerful prevention controls, meaningful detection tools and considerable recovery rights. If you are serious about protecting your identity, then it is your responsibility to learn the applicable portions of the laws and take the appropriate steps. A considerable number of *appropriate steps* are detailed earlier in this book.

 # Chapter 9

Debrief

A quality debriefing is necessary at the end of any mission to tie together loose ends, discuss additional concepts and learn for future missions. The most important component of this debriefing is the recognition that the system has issues, but it is not completely broken. Even if it were *broken*, what choice do you have? Do you want to spend your life upset about a poor identity system, or would you rather determine a few simple things you can do to protect yourself? If you focus on managing the controllable factors, then you are empowered to pursue what's most important in life. I have spent my life analyzing the system to determine these *few simple things* so all you have to do is learn and practice them (it sounds like you got the better end of the bargain on this one).

When someone talks about "identity theft," most of the time they are referring to financial identity theft since it receives the greatest attention and has the most victims. For this same reason, it seems to have the most developed identity theft laws and regulations. With all of these facts, it is particularly perplexing why the credit reporting agencies (CRAs), the epicenter of financial identity theft, have the least accountability and the lowest proportion of identity theft-related costs.

It is possible to make the argument that just like USPS

is the purveyor of mail and not responsible for the contents, the CRAs are similarly the purveyors of information and not responsible for when the information causes harm. However, this argument could not be further from the truth; the USPS actually has a specific department set up to combat crimes committed via mail, including identity theft! In fact, the United States Postal Inspection Service was founded by Benjamin Franklin and is one of the oldest law enforcement agencies in the U.S.

Why does the USPS have a sophisticated, well-run investigation unit with vast resources ($458 million budget for Postal Inspection Service in 2007[75]) while identity theft had $2 million, or $0.18 per victim, in 2009 allocated towards enforcement for the Department of Justice? No offense to the USPS, but how can the integrity of the USPS be so much more important to our infrastructure and our country than our citizens' identity system? The electronic age (and increased competition from other carriers) has diminished the value of the USPS. Comparatively, the value of our identity infrastructure has increased such that the identity ecosystem is of greater importance to our overall system than it has ever been. Without a functional identity infrastructure, you would not likely be able to get a driver's license, open a bank account or receive medical attention. Society as we know it would grind to a halt. Let me explain.

Since its inception in 1775, the USPS has had a single, great principle: "that every person in the United States – no matter who, no matter where – has the right to equal access

---

75   "Management Advisory – Review of Postal Inspection Service." Office of the Inspector General. H. Glen Walker, Chief Financial Officer, Executive Vice President. United States Postal Service. September 21, 2007.

to secure, efficient, and affordable mail service."[76] They have delivered (no pun intended) tremendously on this principle and provided incredible value to our society. In fact, the Constitutional Post, the predecessor to the USPS, had strict security requirements that provided a safe method of communication and played a vital role in achieving American independence. Our founding fathers were able to securely correspond with each other. Without this secure communication, the American Revolution may have never occurred.

However, "in the 20th century and opening years of the 21st centuries, competition grew for every postal product. The rise of electronic communications and other technologies offered alternatives for sending statements, payments, and personal messages."[77] Mail volume was 213 billion in 2006, 177 billion in 2009 and is projected to decrease to 150 billion by 2020.[78] Most of the decrease is in *real*, first class mail (not the junk mail that you will be able to minimize by opting out with the CRAs), and judging by the rate decrease from 2006 to 2009, it appears mail volume will be substantially less than 150 billion by 2020.

On the contrary, identity theft has elevated from an obscure and little-known crime in the 1990s with its first law (Identity Theft Act) passed in 1998, to a crime with 11.1 million adult victims and a cost of $54 billion in 2009 in the U.S. As the 2009 Gallup Crime survey shows, American's

---

76   John E. Potter, Postmaster General. *The United States Postal Service: An American History 1775-2006*. 2007.

77   Ibid. p 57.

78   "Postal Service Outlines 10-Year Plan to Address Declining Revenue, Volume." What They Think? <http://whattheythink.com/news/index.cfm?id=42480>

top-ranked crime concern is identity theft, with 66 percent of U.S. adults saying that they worry "frequently" or "occasionally" about being a victim of identity theft.[79] The statistics clearly prove that identities are significantly more important to our society and for liberty and prosperity than our physical mail. Yet, the entities *primarily* responsible for identity theft (meaning the entities that have the best potential to control identity theft), the CRAs, have done virtually nothing to combat this crime and in fact have taken several steps that actually aggravate the problem.

CRAs aren't completely to blame; they have a responsibility to their stakeholders and aren't required to solve societal issues. It is well known that a lesser amount of secure PII decreases the amount of identity theft. If the CRAs were to institute a rule where consumers had to opt in to receive preapproved offers of credit (instead of the current opt out structure), then this would decrease identity theft; however, it would decrease CRA profitability because the CRAs earn income from selling your PII. Also, why does each CRA offer identity theft detection programs for incorrect or fraudulent information that they are responsible for keeping accurate? A component of the cost of the identity protection service from the CRAs is for insurance. In other words, you are paying the companies offering insurance to help you correct information with those same companies!

If the law dictates it is the CRAs' responsibility to keep accurate records, don't you think anything you do to help them maintain accurate records should be free of charge? In fact, if it is truly the CRAs' legal responsibility to keep accurate records, then they should *pay you* to make certain

---

79   Gallup Crime survey. 2009. <http://www.gallup.com/poll/123713/two-in-three-americans-worry-about-identity-theft.aspx>

the records are accurate! You should be paid if you find mistakes on credit reports by the CRAs. If this were reality, imagine how much care the CRAs would provide to make certain that the identity validation initiated by the creditors is 100 percent accurate. Do you think they would still accept only "seven of nine SSN digits" as acceptable identity validation if they lost money for improper validation? Of course not! But if they do not have *skin in the game* or any penalty for their mistakes, then they will continue to keep making them!

I mentioned that I do not *completely blame* the CRAs for not solving the issue of identity theft, but they certainly do not need to be a major part of the problem. We have already proven that they do not have much care for the validation component from which identity theft springs, but what about when the victim has fraudulent accounts listed on his or her reports? Do the CRAs at least show reasonable care for such clients? No. In fact, the CRAs actually profit from inaccuracies. According to Leonard Burnett's written testimony before the House Committee on Financial Services in 2007:

> *Rather than increase resources and attention to de- velop solutions to these inaccuracy and identity theft problems, the national reporting agencies have cut their per capita resources for resolving consumer disputes at the same time they have rushed to maxi- mize profits for the same. For example, Equifax pays its outsource vendor in the Philippines between $.41 and $.57 to process <u>each consumer dispute letter</u> it receives. But through the agencies' E-Oscar system, they charge no less than $.25 from their creditor cus-*

tomers for each ACDV dispute form sent electroni-
cally. Thus, if a consumer disputes five inaccurate
accounts after a file is mixed or an identity is stolen,
Equifax would pay its vendor a fraction of the gross
amount (e.g., $1.25) it charges its creditor custom-
ers through E-Oscar. In fact, the more automated
disputes it sends out, the more money it generates.[80]

Yes, you read that correctly. The CRAs are earning money for inaccurate information on your report. They do not earn money by confirming that the information is correct. The CRAs have a litany of other abusive practices, but I am trying my best to keep this related to the impact on identity theft. Let it be said that there are so many processes and components of the CRAs that hurt the consumer, and then they smile, collect your money and act like they are on your side. I cannot tell you how many people have said to me, "Why do you think I should trust your practice of setting fraud alerts when I can go to the source of a well-respected company such as (one of the CRAs) and purchase their preventive monitoring product? The guardians of my information certainly know more than you!" That drives me absolutely crazy. It's like a chicken stating that the fox cares about him, even as the fox gnaws on one of the chicken's legs.

Of all of the players within the industry, the CRAs rank just below debt collectors. At least collectors are just *doing their job* and not contributing to identity theft. On the *Horrible-Neutral-Oustanding* scale of effect on identity

---

80   Leonard A. Bennett. Consumer Litigation Associates on behalf of the National Association of Consumer Advocates. Written Testimony Before The House Committee on Financial Services Regarding "Fair Credit Reporting Act: How it Functions for Consumers and the Economy." June 19, 2007.

theft, CRAs fall somewhere between *Horrible* and *Neutral* (and closer to *Horrible*). Using this same scale for effect on mail fraud, the United States Postal Inspection Service is near *Outstanding* (nobody is perfect). In fact, if you had the Postal Inspection Service develop *and* enforce rules relating to identity theft *for the CRAs* (without regard to profit but rules that are deemed *reasonable*), I am certain we could have a 50 percent reduction of identity theft with three years. It is my estimation that the CRAs are in a similar situation as subprime lenders were just prior to the crash: they are enjoying their substantial profits with little regard to unstoppable market forces. The general populace is becoming increasingly *credit educated* and will not tolerate these gross injustices much longer. Once the ball drops, the resulting landscape will be completely different than it is today.

For those from the CRAs reading at this point, you must feel like Phillip Morris after reading a study confirming that smoking causes death.

My approach to this debrief is similar to the *nameless, rankless* debrief. After a fighter jet mission is flown, those involved are included in a debrief *without name or rank*. Safety is the primary concern and the room for error is so thin for fighter pilots that they temporarily suspend the normal military command structure. Whether you are the lowest ranking or the highest ranking in the debrief, you are expected to contribute to the debrief without fear of retribution by a superior officer. I consider identity theft in the same regard. The room for error is minimal and the consequences can be catastrophic. So with that in mind, let's consider the Social Security Administration. The Social Security number is the highest value target because, aside from our biometrics, it is the only truly unique identifier and the Social Security Administration is responsible for issuance. Similar to the CRAs, it is not the SSA's responsibility to solve the identity theft epidemic by themselves. However, the SSA could institute many simple policies that would make the proliferation of identity theft much more difficult. For example, the SSA could make the cards tamper-resistant and phase out previous versions of the card. There are currently over 50 acceptable versions of SS cards. Thieves take the path of least resistance and learning to counterfeit the most recent and secure version is not necessary when they can print a previous version directly from their typewriter.

Well, if the SSA is not going to change its cards or numbering system, maybe it can at least have practices that minimize the fraud and theft. E-Verify is an Internet-based system that compares information from an employer's Form I-9 and Employment Eligibility Verification to data from U.S. Department of Homeland Security and Social Security Administration records to confirm employment eligibility. This form assists employers in legally hiring employees because, according to the Immigration Reform and Control Act of 1986, employers are prohibited from knowingly hiring illegal workers.

Participation in E-Verify is free and optional for most private companies, but the Office of Management and Budget (OMB) mandated that all federal agencies and departments begin verifying their new hires through E-Verify by October 1, 2007. The humor is not lost that a different agency in the government needs to make a mandate for the SSA to use its own program that assists in securing SSNs… wow. It gets better: E-verify was not used by 19 percent of the SSA's new hires in 2008 and 2009 and 49 percent of the *verified* did not appear to be verified as per the time requirements.[81] This is almost beyond comprehension: a primary agency in charge of verifying identity through Social Security numbers is not even participating in its own program! With leadership like this, why would anybody choose to follow?

Just when you think it could not get any worse, try to get assistance from the SSA when someone is illegally using your SSN for employment. I personally investigated this process. Why? Two reasons: 1) I thought someone was using my SSN for employment purposes, and 2) there are no resources that describe what the SSA does when you believe someone is committing Social Security identity theft.

I followed the instructions to the letter.

1. I reviewed my Social Security Statement, and I identified a discrepancy.

2. I called the SS fraud hotline and was referred to a field office.

3. I called the field office and waited on hold for a long time (approximately 15 minutes) before I was dropped. I did not hang up, I was dropped. I repeated the same process.

4. I decided to go into the field office since I could not get assistance via phone. I waited approximately 30 minutes to speak to a representative to explain the situation, and she indicated that I needed to speak to a specialist.

---

81   "The Social Security Administrator's Implementation of the E-Verify Program for New Hires." Office of the Inspector General. Social Security Administration. January 2010.

5. I waited nearly another hour before I was able to speak to a *specialist*.

    a. After explaining the situation, we reviewed the SS Statement and identified the discrepancy.

    b. I asked if we could determine the exact discrepancy within earnings of a specific year. In other words, I could tell it was wrong, but could we get more detailed information of the yearly earnings so we can drill down the issues?

    c. She replied no.

    d. She handed me a tri-fold brochure.

    e. I quickly realized this was the same information online; so, I politely informed her that I was not interested in educating myself, I was interested in opening a case and getting resolution to someone fraudulently using my SSN. I even told her that I believed I knew who it was (I had a reasonable suspicion of someone), and I could provide contact information. She said that there was nothing she could do.

    f. She basically stated that you have extra income reporting, so it was a bank error in my favor in regards to SS benefits (increased earnings means greater benefits) and if I had issue with anybody that it was with the IRS. I informed her that someone was committing SS fraud (not IRS fraud—maybe that too, but that was not my point),

I believed I knew who it was and I would like the SSA to assist.

g. She reiterated that "there was nothing she can do."

Basically, I bring a Social Security fraud/identity theft case wrapped with a bow to the SSA, and they tell me there is nothing they can do. Additionally, I learned there is a SS form titled 7050 Request For Social Security Earnings Information, which provides specific periods and earnings by employer including names and addresses. If you want to find SS fraud/identity theft, 7050 is the document you need. Did I find it on the FTC website? Social Security Administration website? Social Security fraud hotline? Social Security field office? No, no, no, no. I learned about it (and received it from) the Identity Theft Resource Center (*excellent* resource) based on an inquiry I submitted. By the way, the SSA charges $15 or more to provide this report, depending on the number of years you request. Why didn't anybody from the SSA let me know about this form and/or why is this form not listed on the SSA website anywhere near information relating to identity theft? After going through this experience personally, I can only believe that either they do not care or they do not have a division similar to the Postal Inspection Service. By the way, if it is 1099-SS Fraud, then you really have no recourse because this information is not reported directly to the SSA.

Based on the SSA's unwillingness to secure SS cards, incompetence in administrating their own E-Verify program and lack of enforcement for SS-related identity theft cases, it is clear the SSA is not a good agency to partner with in the hopes of minimizing identity theft. The sooner we can get the unique numbering system away from them, the better. Again, I am sure the Postal Inspection Service would determine reasonable rules and enforcement policies to get this under much better control than its current management. Maybe we should start sending these types of cases to the Postal Inspector hoping they can supersede the SSA's authority?[82]

So we have concluded that the two groups with the best ability to minimize incidents and mitigate the negative effects of identity theft (the CRAs and the SSA) basically don't care. Or at least they do not care enough to take any meaningful action.

One would think that there has to be someone or something on your side to protect you. Aside from me, you got nobody. Identity Theft Assistance Center (ITAC) is an organization that many financial institutions use in the case of data breaches. In these cases, ITAC provides "victim assistance and identity management services...at no cost to customers of ITAC member companies."[83] Many of the largest banks are members (e.g., Bank of America, Citigroup, Wells Fargo, etc.). The website makes them appear altruistic, and they even have a ".org" address. The setup of the website is about as altruistic as they get.

I am a consumer of a few of the member institutions, so I sent them the following note:

> Hello – I am a client of a few of your members (BofA and Fidelity), and I am a little confused/have some

---

82   "Identity Theft via the U.S. Mail." United States Postal Inspection Service. <https://postalinspectors.uspis.gov/forms/idtheft.aspx>

83   "Services." Identity Theft Assistance Center. <http://www.identitytheftassistance.org/pageview.php?cateid=48>

questions about your recovery services:

1) does my financial institution need to initiate the request for assistance, or if I think my identity has been stolen, am I entitled to your services?

2) what is included with your recovery services? The website basically provides details of how to recover identity yourself but also states ITAC assists with the recovery? for example – do you set fraud alerts or do I do this myself? If you set them, I read they last 90 days, do you reset them? If I need to reset them, can you provide me instructions?

3) is there a certain period of time you offer your services (how long?)? what happens after?

4) do you assist with recovery of medical identity? if so, how?

I am sorry if these questions seems basic, but I recently noticed medical related bills on my credit report which are not mine, and I am trying to determine what to do next! Thanks for your help!! – DK

They were some pretty basic questions, and I was trying to get a feel for the organization and process. I received the following response:

Thank you for contacting ITAC. Because of the large volume of emails we receive, we are unable to personally respond to each inquiry. If you think you are a victim of identity theft, please visit our consumer pages to find out what you can do to protect yourself.

I was not certain if they were not replying to my e-mail or that they may not be able to reply to my e-mail. Either way, why have a *contact us* option and not have the ability to reply especially when it is a member covered under your service agreement? Potentially I was jumping the gun; so, I replied to their e-mail requesting a reply to inform me if they intend to help.

> Hello,
>
> I am extremely confused! My financial institution is an ITAC member (I can provide proof), and there has been suspicious activity in my account. You are supposed to help me recover my identity, and you are unable to have a real representative answer basic questions? Are you just a self-help, reference organization? If so, it would be nice to know so I am not wasting my time.
>
> Either way, please let me know!
> DK

I did not receive a reply to the above e-mail.

Communication is absolutely essential for any restoration service. Any company that cannot answer e-mails from the "contact us" has an incredibly poor communication apparatus or management. Either way, it is ill-prepared to offer true recovery services. I did not go through the recovery process (since they never replied), but companies like this have a transparent business model. When there is a breach, they provide poor service, but since your member organization offered you a free year subscription to their service, you are hooked on their identity theft product. These prevention products are normally cheap monitoring services. After one year, you are convinced to stay with them and pay because you have already learned first-hand that your information can be compromised.

Not surprisingly, ITAC has a sister for-profit company (ITAC Sentinel) that offers such a service. The lowest price service is $10 per month, and it does not even include credit monitoring. Honestly, I am not sure what it provides other than a credit report and a score. The service that offers credit monitoring is $18 per month. So, your data and/or identity has been compromised via a breach. You receive one free year of this service, and then you feel locked into a rather useless $200-per-year product. Of course, they mis-market their product as fraud prevention when a breach occurs.[84] They are not preventing fraud; they are not even detecting fraud; they are merely indicating account activity. It seems absolutely amazing that some of the largest banks in the world get bamboozled by such simplistic, deceptive advertising. Maybe it is not so amazing considering some of the basic, incompetent management decisions of the last 10 years by these same people that led to the subprime meltdown.

As I have repeatedly mentioned, there are certainly forces out there working against the security of your identity, and many of these forces are surprising. Good or bad, right or wrong, you are ultimately responsible for your identity, and there is no one who has as much vested in your identity than you. Thus, it makes sense that you are primarily responsible for its safekeeping. I suggest acknowledging these evil forces without wasting too much effort dwelling

84   "Data Breaches." Identity Theft Assistance Center. <http://www.identitytheftassistance.org/pageview.php?cateid=73>

on things that are substantially outside of your control. There are plenty of weapons for you to fight back these forces; so, use these weapons (most of which require minimal resource commitment), and chances are that you will be just fine. My final suggestion is to share your comprehensive knowledge of this subject with your friends and family. Reach around your community and take proactive steps. You do not need to always scream from a soapbox, but politely show others the light. A safe identity is a happy identity.

♟ Appendix

A. Identity Ambassador Commission

Educo. Exercito. Munimen. These are Latin for Educate, Train and Protect, and they are also pillars of the Identity Ambassador Commission (IAC). Up until this point, the book has had a laser-like focus on the "Educate" component, and it has been very individually focused. If you educate and train based on the concepts presented in this book (including continuous self-education), then you have the tools to protect yourself. If I have assisted you to reach this point of effective protection for yourself, then I am pleased; however, if you are still reading, then you have an elevated interest and understanding of this topic. While I am pleased you are able to protect yourself, I am thrilled if you decide to take your knowledge and interest of this incredibly important topic and put it to good use by helping others to protect themselves.

Helping others may come in the form of educating guests at a dinner party who are inadvertently practicing detection tactics whilst believing they are practicing preventive tactics (due to deceptive advertising), or it could be conducting training seminars at senior centers (as often it is seniors who are preyed upon and have the least knowledge of the subject). People with an accurate and thorough understanding of this subject are scarce, and the eradication of this awful crime must start with the efforts of these few, which includes you. It is not necessary to join an official group to help others, but if you want to expand your reach or desire a professional identity certification, then the following is intended for you.

Identity theft is a pervasive, costly and misunderstood crime. Lack of credible, current and useful resources has created a knowledge vacuum whereby this crime continues to proliferate with relatively minimal resistance.

The IAC was developed and designed to reverse the identity theft epidemic by empowering citizens through education and training. The IAC has aggregated disparate resources and produced targeted training courses that ultimately provide the best practices for the prevention, detection and recovery from identity theft.

IAC's core belief is that identity theft education has a maximum effectiveness only if it is Free, Accurate, Current, Transparent and Shared (F.A.C.T.S.) by all.

IAC has developed a multi-communal strategy that maximizes the effectiveness and breadth of the message. Training courses have been developed to reach both the online community as well as the local community center. Every Identity Ambassador completes a thorough training course that is substantially similar to the contents of this book. The final examination tests the applicant's mastery of the material. If the applicant passes the examination, then he or she is designated as a Certified Identity Expert (CIE).

Mastery of the material may initially earn the applicant the CIE designation, but to maintain this designation requires adherence to the IAC Code of Ethics, which is based on the F.A.C.T.S. principle.

Due to the considerable misinformation, falsehoods and conflicting motivations by experts within the industry, it is paramount that a Certified Identity Expert maintains the highest degree of integrity, professionalism and knowledge of the identity theft industry.

Identity Ambassador Commission's Code of Ethics

A Certified Identity Expert shall:

1. Provide identity theft training for free. It is acceptable to charge a nominal fee to cover expenses of presentations; however, a CIE shall never profit from identity theft presentations or training.

2. Improve his or her knowledge through continuous education. Identity theft landscape and trends are constantly changing, and it is the responsibility of the CIE to stay at the forefront of the industry through vigilant research and education to ensure the training is accurate, current and relevant.

3. Never make or imply a false claim that any method, technique or service is 100 percent effective. IAC training presentations are intended to educate and provide the tools to substantially decrease the likelihood of identity theft. No technique(s) or service can 100 percent prevent identity theft, and thus no such claims are tolerated.

4. Clearly distinguish between identity theft *prevention*, *detection* and *recovery*. It is common practice for industry players to mischaracterize these three defense categories in order to further personal goals and motivations. Such misinformation contributes

to the confusion within the industry and needlessly elevates identity risk.

5. Never bundle identity theft training with other goods or services. It is understood that many CIEs are financial professionals in closely related fields or potentially affiliates of identity theft companies. It is acceptable to offer these ancillary products at training presentations; however, it is never acceptable to make the purchase of these products mandatory.

6. Never offer identity theft services/products without disclosing the separation between the service and the Identity Ambassador training. To maintain the integrity of the organization and the training, it is necessary to maintain clear lines of separation.

7. Inform consumers of identity theft defense tactics and, if applicable, that the consumer can provide him or herself the same defenses without charge. The main goal of the training is to educate about identity theft and not to trick the consumer into purchasing products from the CIE. If a consumer is educated and is interested in a service as a convenience, then this is acceptable.

8. Only offer products and services that accurately reflect and market the product or service. It is inconsistent and not acceptable to claim to believe in this code and then partner with companies that do not believe in the same principles.

9. Make certain to provide the best identity theft education and training by practicing the F.A.C.T.S.

ideology. There are many interrelated forces and motivations that work against this goal, and it is the CIE's responsibility to identify and either eliminate or mitigate the threats to ensure all are provided the best opportunity to minimize the likelihood of identity theft.

The intent of this book is not to recruit for the Identity Ambassador Commission. This is why I have refrained from even raising the topic until the end of the book. The CIE course has the same concepts and information as contained in the book, and if you have made it this far, then I figured it was worthwhile to at least briefly discuss the program and the opportunity. In addition to the CIE program, the IAC also produces and disseminates a complimentary monthly newsletter for both members and non-members. Subscribing to (and reading) this monthly newsletter substantially achieves the continuous self-education component of the identity theft defense strategy.

I cannot stress enough the terrible impact identity theft is having on our society, and it is well documented. It does not gain as much attention or generate the same awful feelings as when you hear of a violent crime, but the overall impact on society is greater. As a result, there are deaths, suicides, divorces, depression, money lost, foreclosures, college opportunities missed, work truancy and aggravation (to name a few). Combatting identity theft requires personal responsibility, but it also requires a communal outreach effort. The Identity Ambassador Commission was developed to spearhead this outreach effort.

B. Parallels Between the Identity Industry and the Subprime Meltdown

There are eerie similarities between the conditions that led to the subprime meltdown and the current landscape of the identity industry. If we ignore these conditions and do not take the appropriate counteractions, then the resulting identity meltdown will relegate the subprime meltdown to a footnote in history. The following are the main similarities:

1. *Banking* and *identity* are integral components of our overall infrastructure that rely on trust to properly function.

2. New practices and emerging technologies drastically changed the business models of the world's largest industries and exponentially increased risk to the companies. Not only did this jeopardize the financial well-being of companies, but it placed the integrity of the overall system at risk.

3. Non-commensurate allocation of risk and costs for failure.

4. The world's largest corporations provided irrational products that were fueled by greed and short-term returns.

5. There is a lack of adequate legislation and enforcement of existing laws.

6. The populace behaved like an ostrich with its head in the sand. We did not completely understand everything and the complexities of the markets, but it

was abundantly clear that something was not right. We did not demand that action was taken to resolve these huge systemic flaws.

1. *Banking* and *identity* are integral components of our overall infrastructure that rely on trust to properly function.

The banking system is an integral component of our society on several levels. Most importantly, banks act as a trusted intermediary between savers and borrowers. Savers have a safe place to store and access wealth. Borrowers have a trusted and predictable way to obtain financing. Over time, the public trust increased to a level where both savers and investors became dependent on this way of doing business. In such an environment, substantial and rapid changes to the system have dire effects to the consumers and overall populace. For example, if you rely on your savings to purchase groceries every Friday, but one time at the checkout you discover your debit card is not allowing the transaction to be processed even though funds are in the account, then on an individual level, this is an annoyance.

Now, imagine if an entire society goes grocery shopping on Friday and nobody has access to his or her funds. The situation rapidly escalates into a catastrophe. The subprime meltdown led us to the brink of such a catastrophe; systemic failures produced this domino effect. I will consider many of the steps that led to this situation, but the important takeaway is to recognize that an immediate, abrupt change to our banking system completely impacts our way of life. In our current system, the integrity of the banking system is vital to our sustainability.

Identity is an even more critical component of our infrastructure than banking. Every component of our society is based on understanding with whom you are dealing. If a police officer pulls you over, then you want to verify that the person is actually a police officer (and has jurisdiction in the area you are driving). If you are purchasing a hamburger from McDonald's, then you want to know it is actually McDonald's and not McDowell's (like in the movie *Coming to America*). If a bank lends money, then the bank wants to know the individual from whom they expect repayment. *Everything* requires the proper understanding of identities.

If the carpet is pulled out from underneath the banks and they realize that they cannot validate with reasonable certainty the identities of individuals and customers, then the same result will happen as what would have happened in the subprime meltdown: all banking activities would stop and nobody would be able to buy groceries. Identity and validation is a critical component of our overall infrastructure.

2. New practices and emerging technologies drastically changed the business models of the world's largest industries and exponentially increased risk to the companies. Not only did this jeopardize the financial well-being of companies, but it placed the integrity of the overall system at risk.

Banks traditionally were able to lend based upon deposits and reserve requirements, and there were regulations based on best practices or norms developed over time. These regulations were intended to keep the banks from taking exorbitant risks and to prevent closings, which erodes the public trust in the system.

There were a myriad of new creative practices and procedures that allowed banks not to be subject to the "rules of banking," including using "off balance sheet lending," derivatives, Collateralized Debt Obligations (CBO), Commercial Mortgage Back Securities (CMBS), offshore accounts and Qualified Special Purpose Entities (QSPE). This creative pattern of deception led the banks to overleverage themselves, which brought with it unregulated and immeasurable risk. Overleveraging meant that even a small correction brings down the entire company. If enough banks are conducting business in a similar manner (as was the case in the subprime meltdown), then a small correction brings down the entire system!

Identities have always been valuable, but creating profitable crime syndicates based on identity theft was not viable until new technologies became embedded into society. I define this point as "when risk went viral." The clearest example is the case of data breaches. Prior to electronic storage of identities, it was quite expensive to steal identities. If every identity stolen required a physical document to track, then it is evident how this is cost prohibitive. To the contrary, one single criminal organization breached 45.7 million data records at T.J. Maxx. From a criminal's perspective, this is a situation with incomprehensible economies of scale.

In the case of skimmers, this is made possible by electronic transference of money. Facebook provides thieves considerable personally identifying information at their fingertips that is easily accessible and free. All of these (and many, many more) technological comforts also provide increased opportunities to identity thieves.

Both the subprime lending industry and the identity industry had market disturbers that significantly changed the industry business models and increased risk to the system. Banks became unlicensed securities brokers. Identities became invaluable commodities that were relatively easy to access, steal and sell. Both cases result in immeasurable and uncontainable risk to our system, which inevitably leads to a drastic and harsh market correction.

3. Non-commensurate allocation of risk and costs for failure.

Risk was not spread appropriately amongst parties based on their return potential and accountability for the final result. Additionally, when the risk resulted in losses, the losses were not fairly distributed as parties that had the least influence on the decisions bared a disproportionately high amount of the losses.

In the banking system, there were many different parties with risk, but when there was failure, the failure was not adequately distributed. When these large investment banks failed, they required a government bailout via TARP (Troubled Asset Relief Program). This is a clear sign that they did not adequately share in the risk. Additionally, there were many deceptive practices that hid the risk (e.g., selling securities to themselves but masquerading as other entities).

This non-commensurate allocation of risk is obvious in the identity industry as well. The credit reporting agencies (CRAs) are primarily responsible for validating identities. However, if they are wrong, they share none of the pain. As I covered in this book, it is possible for a CRA to validate an identity with only seven of nine correct Social Security numbers; however, when this leads to an erroneous conclusion, they suffer no financial consequence.

The CRAs have practices that allow for erroneous

personally identifying information to end up on your credit report, which allows identity theft to proliferate. Yet, there are no financial costs for the CRAs having this erroneous PII. In fact, it is nearly impossible to have the erroneous information removed, even with appropriate supporting documentation, such as a driver's license and Social Security card. The inequitable distribution of risk leads to policies that make identity theft more prevalent!

In the Credit Card Issuer Fraud Management Report by Equifax, credit card losses attributed to fraud are approximately $1 billion, or 1.2 percent of issuer expenses. However, this report states, "the direct costs of fraud attributable in some way to U.S. credit cards could easily exceed $16 billion."[85] This is approximately 20 percent of the overall issuer expenses! This indicates that approximately 94 percent of losses attributable to fraud are unreported. This statistic sounds very similar to the "unreported" transactions in the subprime debacle.

If parties in a system are not commensurately assigned risk and all parties do not understand the risk, then ultimately practices develop that jeopardize the individuals and the overall system.

4. The world's largest corporations provided irrational products that were fueled by greed and short-term returns.

In banking and lending, there are five components utilized in loan decisions (often referred to as the 5 C's of banking):

Character – this refers to the willingness of the bor-

---

85   Credit Card Issuer Fraud Management Report. Mercator Advisory Group. December 2008. <http://www.sas.com/news/analysts/mercator_fraud_1208.pdf>

rower to repay the loan.

Capacity – the ability to repay a loan.

Capital – this is the money you are personally investing or have available to support the loan.

Collateral – this is the security supporting the loan in case of default.

Condition – this refers to the national and local economy, the industry and the bank itself.

In the residential lending industry, character was assumed to be *Good* (on a scale of *Bad–Fair–Good–Excellent*) for two reasons: 1) Due to the massive volume of loans, it was impossible for an underwriter to judge the character of each and every borrower and 2) this process is highly subjective and would inevitably lead to violations of the Equal Credit Opportunity Act. How can an underwriter judge and support that one individual seems more likely to repay the debt than another?

Condition was also assumed to be *Very Good*. The banks were using models that were considering 3–7 percent of real estate or collateral appreciation. Additionally, conditions in the bank were not accurately reflected in portfolio distribution. For example, banks were not considering "what if there is overall market depreciation or what if the secondary markets dry up for this sort of product, do I have a reasonable out?" They could have lessened exposure to a point where "the out" was tough but manageable. This sort of thinking allowed for loans that were above the value of the actual houses themselves, e.g., 125 percent loan-to-value (LTV) loans. The prevailing thought was that the market was appreciating fast enough that, even with a certain level of default, there was enough collateral that the losses were acceptable. However, when an assumed 3–7 percent increase changes to a 10 percent decrease, the house of cards comes tumbling down.

Capacity measured the borrower's credit and ability to repay. Most lenders were using a FICO classic scoring model and using the results from the three credit reporting agencies to determine credit. This provided a snapshot of a borrower's previous payment history, which was supposed to be a solid indicator of future payment history.

FICO scores range from 300–850, with the higher scores indicating a better credit profile and likelihood of repayment. Loans were being commonly extended to borrowers with scores down to 500 FICO, which according to FICO included all but 2 percent of those with scores! In other words, 98 percent of the people qualified for mortgage loans. This does not seem like very reasonable lending standards!

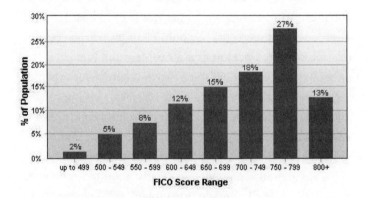

National Distribution of FICO Scores[86]

---

86   "National Distribution of FICO Scores." Bankrate and MyFICO. com. <http://www.bankrate.com/finance/credit-cards/fico-score-over-780-is-good-enough.aspx>

To raise the ante, banks came up with "no score" programs (some of these programs were necessary because the government forced banks into the Community Reinvestment Act, which meant extending credit to underserved markets). This means that a borrower who had not even opened up a $1,000 credit card (and most likely would not qualify for such a credit card) probably would be eligible for a $200,000 loan. I support the idea of homeownership and bringing products to underserved markets, but this is the equivalent of putting a brand new driver in a Ferrari before learning how to drive a Yugo. Is there no middle ground? Is residential lending the appropriate social testing platform? Apparently not.

The other part of capacity is the ability to repay, which is neatly represented in debt-to-income ratio. There are various manners to determine this ratio, but a simple equation is to divide the total monthly housing expenses (principal, interest, taxes and insurance) by gross income. The lenders had pushed this ratio up to 55 percent (I even heard of cases of accepting 60 percent). To put this in proper perspective, this means that a person in a 30 percent tax bracket would only have 15 percent left over for *all* other living expenses, including utilities, repairs, food, car, car insurance, cell phone, entertainment, gas, etc. You do not need to take an advanced class in econometrics to determine that such a ratio does not make sense and is not sustainable.

Capital is the amount personally invested and/or the down payment. I already mentioned 125 percent LTV loans, but those were somewhat niche products. On the contrary, 100 percent LTV loans were commonplace. In fact, these loans commonly allowed for "seller contributions," which meant that somebody could purchase a house with literally none of their own money. These loans were sold on the secondary market, but these loans were also supported by the Federal Housing Authority (commonly 97 percent LTV with 6 percent seller contributions led to "no money down"). Without considering any of the other variables, why would you make a loan to somebody that has no "skin in the game"? They have nothing to risk because none of their own money went into the transaction. At the first sign of trouble, they are leaving the loan because they have very little deterrent not to walk away.

There were also many loans that required no reserves or those where you could "state" how much you have in case there is a disruption to cash flows. As a lender, you want to know if someone loses his or her job that he or she is not skipping the mortgage payment the very next month.

Collateral in the case of residential lending is very similar to capital, and we have adequately covered this topic for the purposes of this book.

I attempted not to go into too great of detail regarding the subpar lending practices. There were many, many more irrational products, but the examples provided demonstrate to someone with little or no banking background how incredibly and unquestionably irrational these products were. The next questions are commonly "why" and "how"? Why did they make these loans, and how did they stay profitable for so long while making such idiotic decisions?

The new practices discussed in the second point, the non-commensurate risk allocation covered in the third point and greed allowed this to happen. First, the bankers became brokers to the secondary market. If the loans were "performing" well, then they got as many of them as they could. Banking principles no longer mattered because the only way to maximize profit was to package the loans and sell them as quickly as possible. Banks forgot that they were actually banks. The way to outperform your peers was to come up with new, innovative products that pushed the risk standard or limits. The secondary markets were insurance companies, foreign capital and pension funds with no real expertise in residential banking (although they pretended). They were lured by exorbitant returns and greed. All of the parties were viewing the market based on short-term return and not sound lending principles.

The irrational banking products of the early to mid-2000s are now well documented, but there exist similar, irrational products in the identity theft industry. Unfortunately, the overall identity industry is not quite as well developed as the lending industry and does not have simple-to-understand models such as the 5 C's of lending.

It is necessary to understand that the CRAs are responsible for accurately reporting (or taking reasonable steps to accurately report) information in your report. Remember, you are not hiring or electing them to report your information; so, with this understanding, the government developed rules to protect you from irresponsible practices. If you were electing their services, then you could cancel such service if they were not accurate. With this understanding, here are the most egregious violations of the rational product rule:

    a) An "accuracy detection" product. The CRAs are responsible for making certain your information is accurate. Instead of paying you to help them fulfill this responsibility, you have to pay them for what they fancifully refer to as "credit monitoring"?

b) Identity theft insurance. They control whether your identity is stolen (they can refuse to validate without proper information) and certainly they are responsible for the accuracy of the information contained in your report. Why do you need insurance to cover their responsibility? If anything, they should purchase the insurance in case they make a mistake.

c) Fight against automatic fraud alerts by third-party providers. If the CRAs are responsible for the accuracy of information on your report, then why would they EVER argue against anything that helps ensure accuracy? The answer to this is simple: they do not care because they do not commensurately share in the losses. Doing the "right thing" is trumped by corporate returns.

This is a very obvious pattern of deception and abuse by the very companies that are supposed to be protecting you. They have literally pulled the wool over all of society. Imagine if a judge were bonused based on the number of convictions he or she handed down—this is close to the current state of affairs with the CRAs and identities. The main difference is the judge is supposed to be impartial and the CRAs are supposed to be on our side—so, the current state is even more egregious than the example.

The specifics of irrational products are different between the lending and identity industries, but the main similarity is that the products are overtly counterintuitive. The irrationality is crystal clear and really appalling.

5. There is a lack of adequate legislation and enforcement of existing laws.

It is impossible to legislate all behavior, and crooks are always seeking to exploit loopholes. The fact that banks, investment banks and hedge funds were acting in a banking capacity but were operating outside the rules of banking demonstrates either a lack of adequate legislation or enforcement, and it was both. On a consumer level, criminals were able to act for a long period of time with windfall returns and minimal fear of getting caught due to lack of enforcement. I discussed in the introduction how the FBI did not have the expertise or manpower to enforce existing laws. I had full cases ready to go, but they simply were not able to take the cases. At the time, it was not sexy to prosecute lending fraud because their focus was on terrorism (this was definitely a good focus, but it is not a "one or the other" proposition). They certainly were not willing to look into cases that were not huge cases. This was a criminal's wonderland.

In the identity industry, the laws are much more confusing and the responsibility for enforcement is not as well defined. This ambiguity presents a larger challenge and more risk to society. When I went into a Social Security office and informed them that there has been Social Security fraud, and they said there was nothing they could do about it, I felt like I was repeating 2005 with the FBI. What do you mean "there is nothing you can do about it"? People are committing serious and obvious violations of the law, which threatens our entire system, and you are unable to enforce the existing laws (which are barely adequate)?

In 2005 the crooks had become so bold that they were

advertising mortgage fraud in ethnic newspapers. Fast-forward to 2010 and there was an enormous identity theft crime ring (over 300 agents involved in the investigation) that was advertising identity theft in a Korean-language newspaper (in the U.S.). Is it coincidence that prior to the meltdown the crooks had become so brazen due to lack of fear of enforcement that they were actually publicly advertising their criminal services? I think not.

6. The populace behaved like an ostrich with its head in the sand. We did not completely understand everything and the complexities of the markets, but it was abundantly clear that something was not right. We did not demand that action was taken to resolve these huge, obvious systemic flaws.

During the build up to the subprime meltdown, there were many things we did not understand. Maybe it was credit default swaps or derivative trading, but we understood that our valet had a nice primary residence, a vacation home in Florida and a few investment properties. I have nothing against the valet industry, but the income level of such a profession did not match the asset level (sure, you can work hard for a long time, save, buy distressed properties, fix them up, etc., but this is not the type of case I am referring to). We knew it did not make sense for people to have nothing "invested" in their "investment" (100 percent LTV). We knew that somebody that did not qualify for a credit card should not be eligible for a major loan (assuming sound lending principles for both). We knew it did not make sense, but we thought, "Oh well, what can I do about it?"

The same holds true in the current state of the identity

industry. We know it is not right that there have been more than 500 million documented data breaches since 2005. We know it is not right that one in seven Social Security numbers are assigned to more than one person. We know that the companies primarily responsible for protecting our identities are profiting from the identity theft industry. We know it is not right that 94 percent of credit card losses attributed to fraud are unreported. *We know all of these things!*

During the build up to the subprime meltdown, we had a plausible defense, as we had never lived through such an event. Behaving like an ostrich was somewhat acceptable because nobody really understood the true extent of the correction. We are now living with the consequences, and we probably have much more to go.

This excuse is not acceptable with the identity meltdown because we understand the consequences of systemic failures to our infrastructure. The longer this is allowed to continue, the harder it will be to recover. If the subprime meltdown occurred in 2003, then the pain would have been minor and recovery short. But, because it continued so long, the stakes were raised, and both pain and recovery increased considerably.

The longer we allow the identity problem to continue without effectively enforcing existing laws and developing adequate new legislation, we will suffer a fate worse than the subprime meltdown.

It is our decision: do we want to piggyback the subprime meltdown with the identity meltdown?

C. Cease and Desist Letter

Date

YOUR FIRST AND LAST NAME
123 Your Address
City, State Zip

COLLECTION AGENCY NAME
123 Collection Agency Address
City, State Zip

RE: Account #: XXXX-XXX-XXXX

To Whom It May Concern:

I request that you CEASE and DESIST in your efforts to collect on the above-referenced account.

I am exercising my right under the Fair Debt Collection Practices Act demanding you to cease further communications.

You are hereby instructed to cease collection efforts immediately or face legal sanctions under applicable federal and state law.

Regards,

Your Name